HOW TO PLAY THE GUITAR

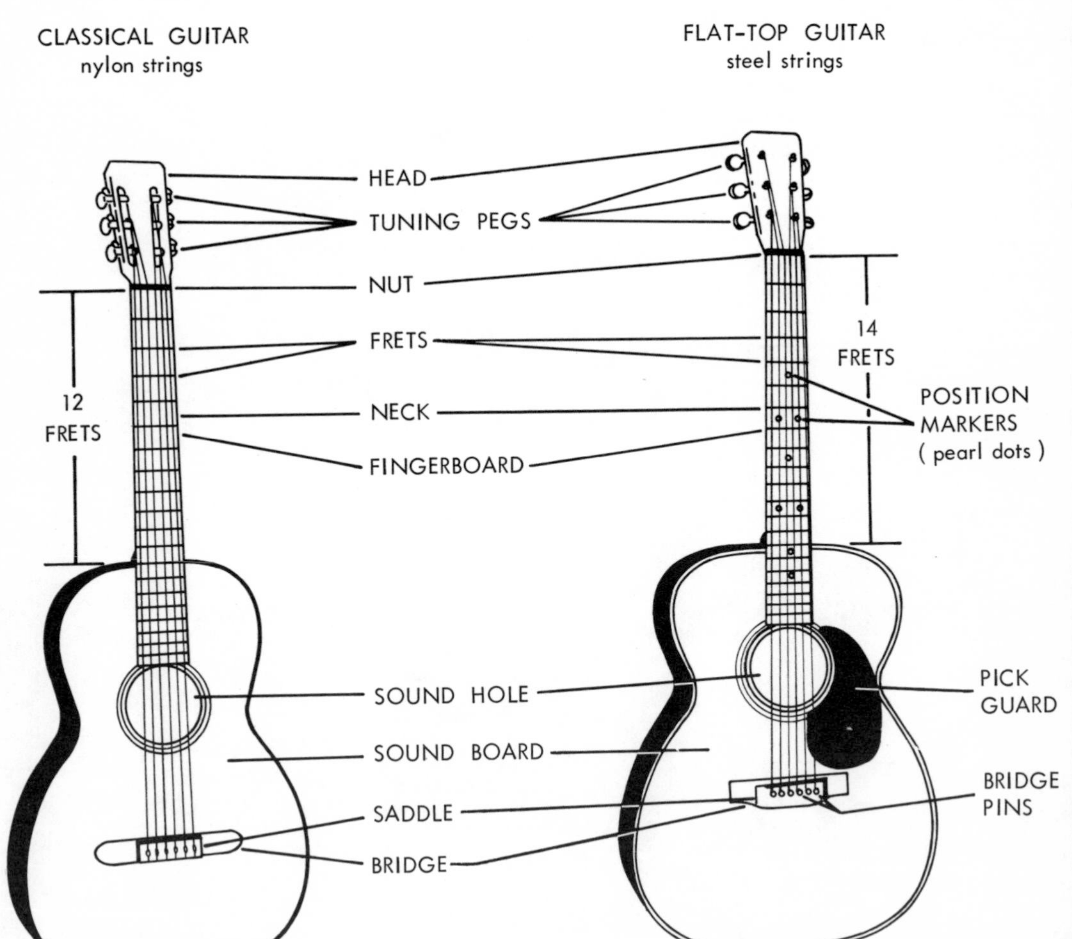
CLASSICAL GUITAR
nylon strings
FLAT-TOP GUITAR
steel strings
HEAD
TUNING PEGS
NUT
FRETS
NECK
FINGERBOARD
12
FRETS
14
FRETS
POSITION
MARKERS
(pearl dots)
SOUND HOLE
SOUND BOARD
SADDLE
BRIDGE
PICK
GUARD
BRIDGE
PINS
END PIN

HOW TO PLAY THE GUITAR

FOLK · BLUES · CALYPSO

Jerry Silverman

DOLPHIN BOOKS
DOUBLEDAY & COMPANY, INC.
GARDEN CITY, NEW YORK

DOLPHIN EDITION: 1973
ORIGINALLY PUBLISHED BY DOUBLEDAY & COMPANY, INC., 1968

ISBN: 0-385-09862-6

PRINTED IN THE UNITED STATES OF AMERICA
20 19 18 17 16

CONTENTS

SECTION ONE: IN THE BEGINNING THERE WAS THE CHORD

Section Two: ARPEGGIOS

Section Three: HAMMERING-ON

SECTION FOUR: THE BANJO BRUSH

SECTION FIVE: BASS RUNS

Section Six: BLUES

Section Seven: CALYPSO AND LATIN RHYTHMS

Section Eight: NOTE READING

A WORD FROM THE AUTHOR

THIS book presents a survey of basic folk guitar techniques. Depending on the student, it may be approached either with or without a teacher. In the latter instance it is desirable, wherever possible, to have some contact with the living world of folk music—even if only through recordings. A friend with a guitar with whom one can literally compare notes is an invaluable asset in pursuing this course of study.

Daily practice—especially in the beginning stages—is of the utmost importance. Unused wrist and finger muscles have to be limbered up and slight calluses must develop on the fingertips of the left hand before the beautiful tone of the guitar can really be produced.

Moving from one chord to another—so awkward a process in the first few weeks—will also become smoother and faster in direct proportion to the amount of time spent in practicing the changes.

With all this, though, the guitar, perhaps more than any other instrument, offers the most *immediate* musical satisfaction. The average student is able to play the first two chords and sing the first couple of songs reasonably well after the very first lesson. Then each new chord and playing technique adds new dimension to your ever-increasing repertoire of songs.

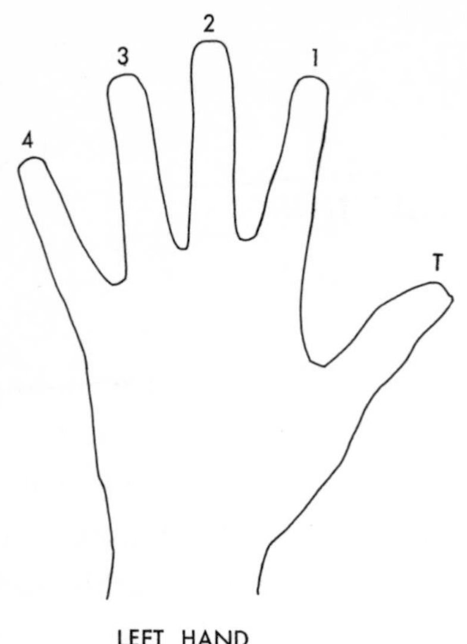

LEFT HAND

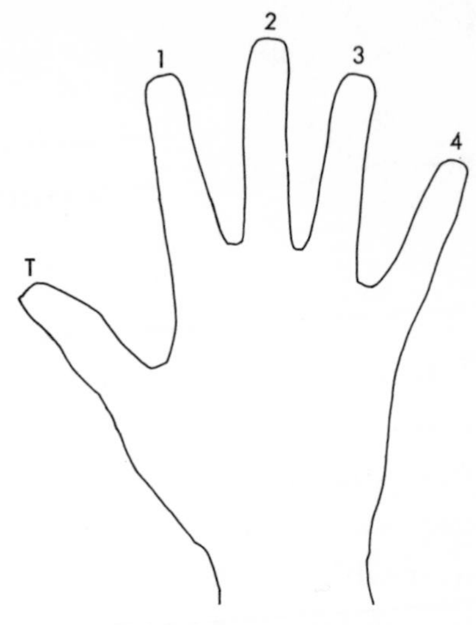

RIGHT HAND

SECTION ONE

IN THE BEGINNING THERE WAS THE CHORD

Fingers, Strings, and Diagrams

The fingers of the left hand press down on the strings at particular frets, depending upon the note or chord desired. The left thumb is rarely used in playing but is customarily pressed against the back of the neck of the guitar for support.

The fingers of the right hand (including the thumb) are used in various combinations to strike the strings. Generally, the strings are played directly over the sound hole. However, interesting variations of tonal quality are obtained by playing nearer the bridge.

The fingers of the right and left hands are numbered as shown on the opposite page.

The guitar may be played in a seated or standing position.

The six strings of the guitar are tuned to the following notes (see Section Eight for a more complete discussion of note-reading):

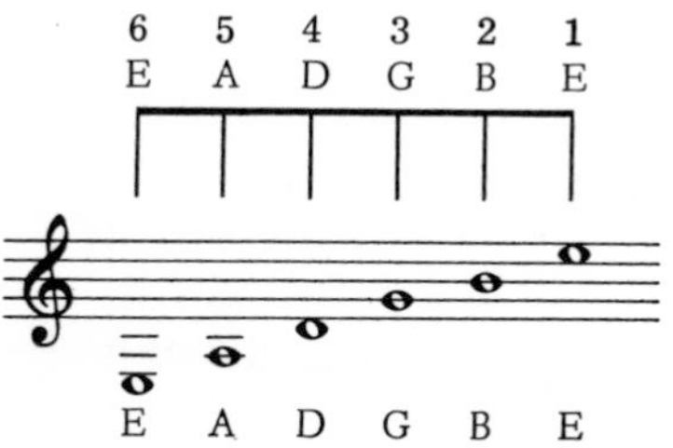

In accordance with customary procedure regarding string instruments, the string with the highest pitch—the thinnest—is numbered "one" (on the guitar, E). The lowest pitch string—the thickest—is "six" (also E, but two octaves lower than the first string).

To learn chords and other folk guitar techniques, the chord diagram method is by far the best and the easiest. The chord diagram is a bird's-eye view of the fingerboard of the guitar, showing clearly the strings and the frets and the places we are to put our fingers (of the left hand).

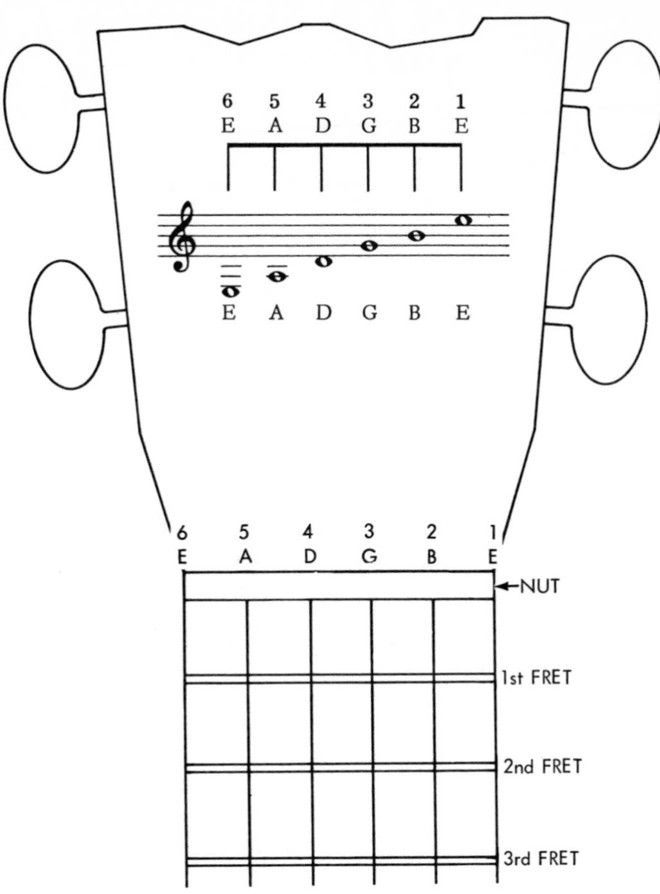

The Key of D Major – Thumb Strum

We will now learn our first two chords using this chord diagram system:

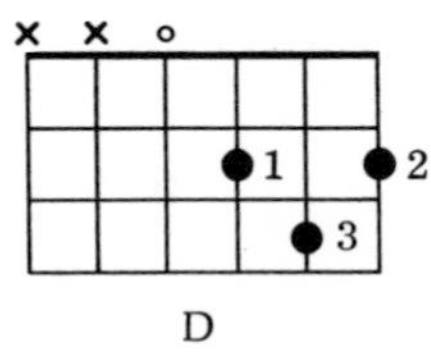

To play the D chord properly—that is, without muffling the strings or producing a buzz—you must press down hard with your fingertips as close to the frets as possible *without actually touching the frets,* as shown in the diagram. Long fingernails on the left hand will be a definite hindrance to the proper playing of chords—for obvious reasons. A zero in the diagram over an open (unfingered) string means that that string is to be played by the right hand along with the rest of the chord. An × indicates that a particular string should not be played.

Therefore, you see that in the D chord the first four strings (D,G,B,E) are to be played together.

Strum (*brush*) downward over these strings with your right thumb. What do you hear? Do you hear four distinct, clear notes or are some of the strings muffled or "dead"? If, say, the first string doesn't sound clearly it may be that your third finger (which should be on the B string) is sort of "leaning over" and touching the E string. That'll kill it every time. You've got to straighten up those fingers and press down vertically, avoiding all but the string you're supposed to be playing.

Chords generally go together in sets, or keys. We'll be talking more about this later. A chord that is often played in conjunction with D is A7.

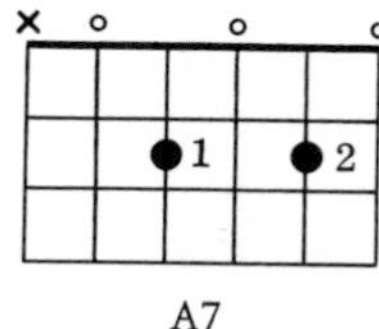

A7

With the A7, you play the first five strings. Again, be careful about muffling the open strings. Also, try to get a clear sound out of the notes on the fourth (D) and second (B) strings. Press close to the second fret on both these strings. Your fingertips will gradually develop the necessary calluses if you practice often. Then they won't hurt any more. Practice, practice, practice . . .

For example: Play D four times slowly with the thumb. Then switch to the A7 and play four times slowly with the thumb. Go back to D and repeat the operation. Practice switching back and forth between these chords several times. Notice the position of the first and second fingers as they play the D chord and how they move just one string apiece—maintaining the same relative position—when they play the A7.

Now we are ready for our first song.

The best way to approach a song in the beginning of your study is to start playing the first chord of that song (in this case, D) at the same speed (*tempo*) that you intend to sing the song. Don't start singing until you have played at least four strums of your "introduction." This intro will, hopefully, give you the starting note of the song (assuming you know the song to begin with). Then, when you start singing, don't play on every syllable you sing, but try to maintain an even, steady beat. When the chords change you may have to slow down a little at first—but with practice (there's that word again) you will soon be able to make a smooth transition from one chord to another without losing a beat.

Follow the diagonal lines over the music—they indicate where you should play.

He's Got the Whole World in His Hands

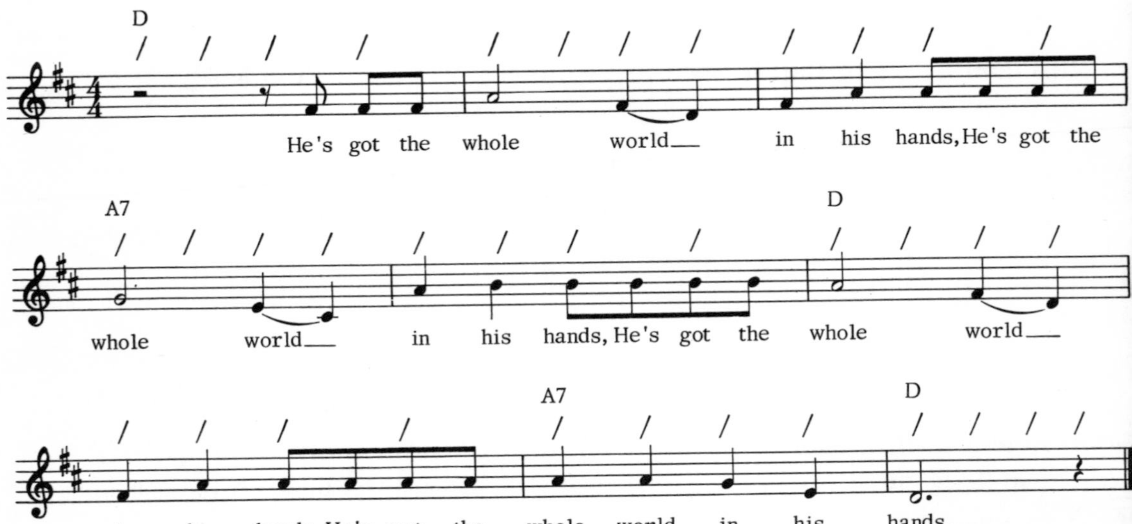

In subsequent verses chords change at the same place in the music that they change in the first verse. This is true of all songs.

D
He's got the wind and the rain in His hands,
A7
He's got the sun and the moon in His hands,
D
He's got the wind and the rain in His hands—
A7 D
He's got the whole world in His hands.

D
He's got you and me, brother, in His hands,
A7
He's got you and me, brother, in His hands,
D
He's got you and me, brother, in His hands—
A7 D
He's got the whole world in His hands.

D
He's got the little bitty baby in His hands,
A7
He's got the little bitty baby in His hands,
D
He's got the little bitty baby in His hands—
A7 D
He's got the whole world in His hands.

D
He's got everybody in His hands,
A7
He's got everybody in His hands,
D
He's got everybody in His hands,
A7 D
He's got the whole world in His hands.

Repeat Verse One

Try the same kind of strumming with *Ten Little Indians.*

Ten Little Indians

D
One little, two little, three little Indians,
A7
Four little, five little, six little Indians,
D
Seven little, eight little, nine little Indians—
A7 D
Ten little Indian boys.

D
Ten little, nine little, eight little Indians,
A7
Seven little, six little, five little Indians,
D
Four little, three little, two little Indians—
A7 D
One little Indian boy.

A Little Rhythm, Professor – The Bass-Chord Strum

Finger a D chord. Pluck just the D string with your thumb—then strum down over the first three strings (B,G,E). Repeat that a few times.

Finger A7. Pluck the A string with your thumb—then strum down over the first four strings (D,G,B,E). Repeat.

This "bass-chord" strum introduces our first sense of rhythmic variety. Prior to this strum every beat was the same. Now we have a feeling of "one-two, one-two . . ." That is, "bass-chord, bass-chord . . ." The first beat of this one-two combination is called the *downbeat.* The second beat is the *upbeat.* The downbeat is the stronger beat, the heavier accent. It is the "left foot" in the parade.

The first word of a song is *not necessarily the downbeat.* In playing with this strum it is more important than ever to begin playing before you begin singing. Then, the natural stresses of the first few words of the song will become apparent and you can start singing on the right beat. In *Polly Wolly Doodle,* the first word, "I" is an upbeat ("two") and the second word "went" is the downbeat ("one"). You'll have to decide for yourself where the beats fall in the other verses. They aren't necessarily like the first.

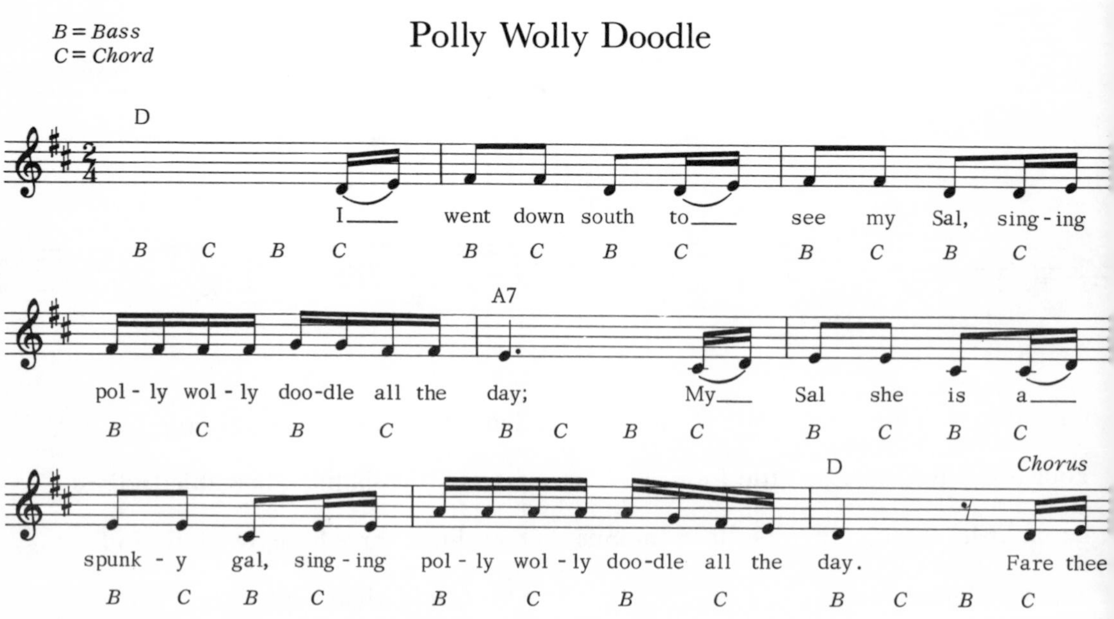

A7
well, Fare thee well, Fare thee well my fair - y fey, For I'm
B C B C B C B C B C B C B C B C
goin' to Lou' - si - an - a for to see my Su - si - an - na, sing - ing
B C B C B C B C
D
pol - ly wol - ly doo - dle all the day.
B C B C B C B C

D
Oh, my Sal, she is a maiden fair,
A7
Sing polly-wolly-doodle all the day;
With curly eyes and laughing hair,
D
Sing polly-wolly-doodle all the day.

Chorus

D
Oh, I went to bed, but it wasn't no use,
A7
Sing polly-wolly-doodle all the day;
My feet stuck out for a chicken roost,
D
Sing polly-wolly-doodle all the day.

Chorus

D
Oh, a grasshopper sitting on a railroad track,
A7
Sing polly-wholly-doodle all the day;
A-picking his teeth with a carpet tack,
D
Sing polly-wolly-doodle all the day.

Chorus

D
Behind the barn, down on my knees,
A7
Sing polly-wolly-doodle all the day;
I thought I heard a chicken sneeze,
D
Sing polly-wolly-doodle all the day.

Chorus

D
He sneezed so hard with the whooping cough,
A7
Sing polly-wolly-doodle all the day;
He sneezed his head and tail right off,
D
Sing polly-wolly-doodle all the day.

Chorus

Most songs need more than two chords.
The chord which most often goes with D and A7 is G.

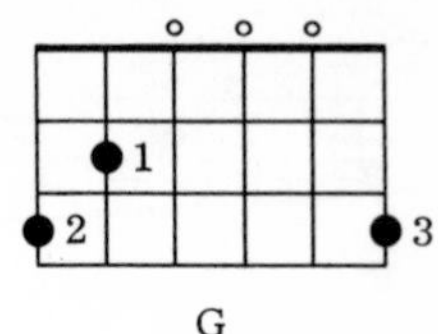

G

The Boll Weevil also starts on an upbeat.

The Boll Weevil

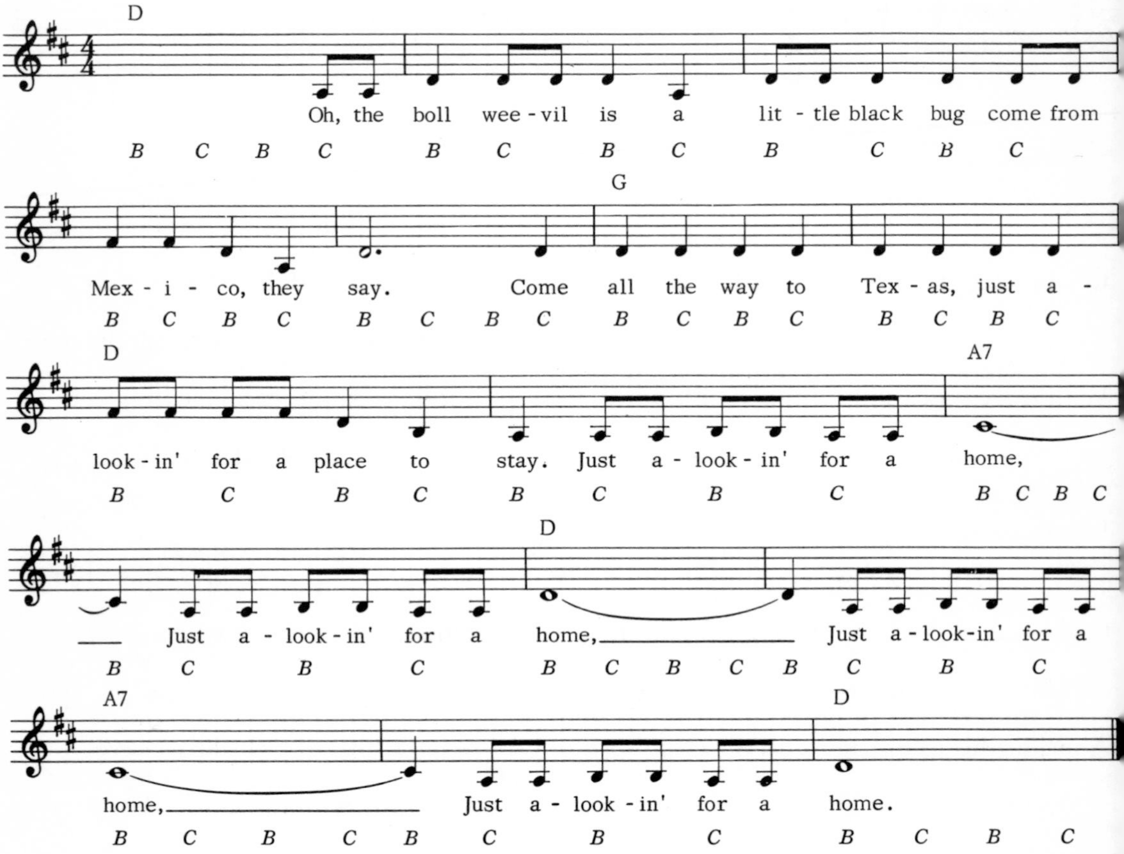

D
Oh, the boll wee - vil is a lit - tle black bug come from
B C B C B C B C B C B C

G
Mex - i - co, they say. Come all the way to Tex - as, just a -
B C B C B C B C B C B C B C B C

D A7
look - in' for a place to stay. Just a - look - in' for a home,
B C B C B C B C B C B C

D
— Just a - look - in' for a home, — Just a - look-in' for a
B C B C B C B C B C B C

A7 D
home, — Just a - look - in' for a home.
B C B C B C B C B C B C

D
The first time I seen the boll weevil,

He was sitting on the square.

G
The next time I seen the boll weevil,

D
He had all his family there—

A7 D
Just a-looking for a home, just a-looking for a home.

A7 D
Just a-looking for a home, just a-looking for a home.

D
The farmer said to the weevil,
"What makes your face so red?"
G
The weevil said to the farmer,
D
"It's a wonder I ain't dead—
A7 D
Just a-looking for a home, just a-looking for a home.
A7 D
Just a-looking for a home, just a-looking for a home."

D
The farmer took the boll weevil,
And he put him in hot sand.
G
The weevil said, "This is mighty hot,
D
But I'll stand it like a man—
A7 D
This'll be my home, this'll be my home.
A7 D
This'll be my home, this'll be my home."

D
The farmer took the boll weevil,
And he put him in a lump of ice.
G
The boll weevil said to the farmer,
D
"This is mighty cool and nice,
A7 D
It'll be my home, it'll be my home.
A7 D
It'll be my home, it'll be my home."

D
The farmer took the boll weevil,
And he put him in the fire.
G
The boll weevil said to the farmer,
D
"This is just what I desire—
A7 D
This'll be my home, this'll be my home.
A7 D
This'll be my home, this'll be my home."

D
The boll weevil said to the farmer,

"You better leave me alone;
G
I ate up all your cotton,
D
And I'm starting on your corn—
A7 D
I'll have a home, I'll have a home.
A7 D
I'll have a home, I'll have a home."

D
The merchant got half the cotton,

The boll weevil got the rest.
G
Didn't leave the farmer's wife
D
But one old cotton dress—
A7 D
And it's full of holes, and it's full of holes.
A7 D
And it's full of holes, and it's full of holes.

D
The farmer said to the merchant,

"We're in an awful fix;
G
The boll weevil ate all the cotton up
D
And left us only sticks—
A7 D
We got no home, we got no home.
A7 D
We got no home, we got no home."

D
The farmer said to the merchant,

"We ain't made but one bale,
G
And before we'll give you that one,
D
We'll fight and go to jail—
A7 D
We'll have a home, we'll have a home.
A7 D
We'll have a home, we'll have a home."

D
And if anybody should ask you

Who was it made this song;
G
It was the farmer man
D
With all but his blue jeans gone—
A7 D
A-looking for a home, a-looking for a home.
A7 D
A-looking for a home, a-looking for a home.

Come and Go With Me starts on a downbeat.

Come and Go With Me

D G D
There ain't no bowing in that land, ain't no bowing in that land,
A7
Ain't no bowing in that land where I'm bound.
D G D
There ain't no bowing in that land, ain't no bowing in that land,
A7 D
Ain't no bowing in that land where I'm bound.

D G D
There ain't no kneeling in that land, ain't no kneeling in that land,
A7
Ain't no kneeling in that land where I'm bound.
D G D
There ain't no kneeling in that land, ain't no kneeling in that land,
A7 D
Ain't no kneeling in that land where I'm bound.

D G D
There's peace and freedom in that land, peace and freedom in that land,
A7
Peace and freedom in that land where I'm bound.
D G D
There's peace and freedom in that land, peace and freedom in that land,
A7 D
Peace and freedom in that land where I'm bound. *Repeat Verse One*

Some songs have more than three chords.

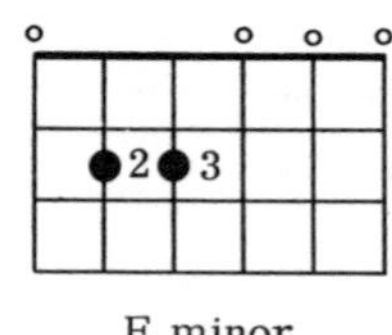

E minor

Michael, Row the Boat Ashore

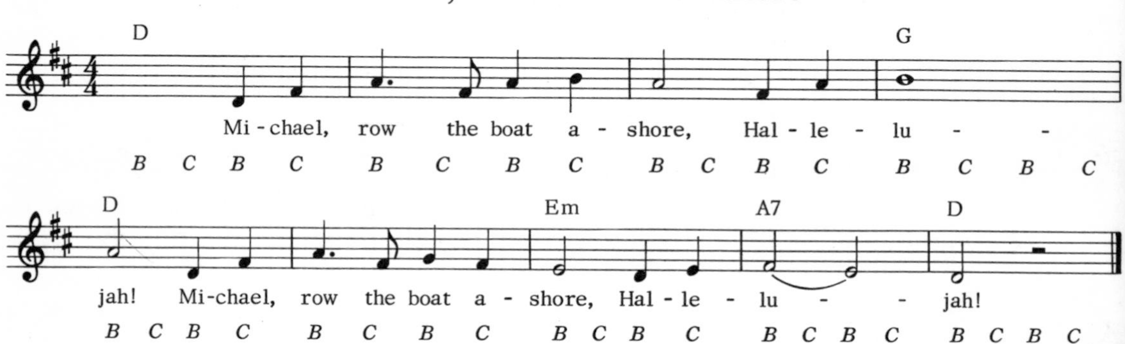

D
Sister, help to trim the sail,
G D
Hallelujah!
Em
Sister, help to trim the sail,
A7 D
Hallelujah!

D
Michael's boat is a gospel boat,
G D
Hallelujah!
Em
Michael's boat is a gospel boat,
A7 D
Hallelujah!

D
Jordan's River is chilly and cold,
G D
Hallelujah!
Em
Chills the body but warms the soul,
A7 D
Hallelujah!

D
Jordan's River is deep and wide,
G D
Hallelujah!
Em
Meet my mother on the other side,
A7 D
Hallelujah!

D
If you get there before I do,
G D
Hallelujah!
Em
Tell my people I'm coming too,
A7 D
Hallelujah! *Repeat Verse One*

Thumb and Finger-Pluck

We come now to a very important step forward. No longer will we use just the right thumb to play the chords. The first three fingers of the right hand will now be used in a basic plucking-type strum. The thumb will continue to strike the bass strings of the chords and the first three fingers will pluck the first three strings, as follows:

Finger an E minor chord.

With the wrist hanging down in a *relaxed* position over the sound hole rest the thumb on the sixth string. Slightly curl the first three fingers toward the strings so that the index finger lightly touches the underside of the third (G) string, the second finger touches the second string (B) and the third finger touches the first string (E).

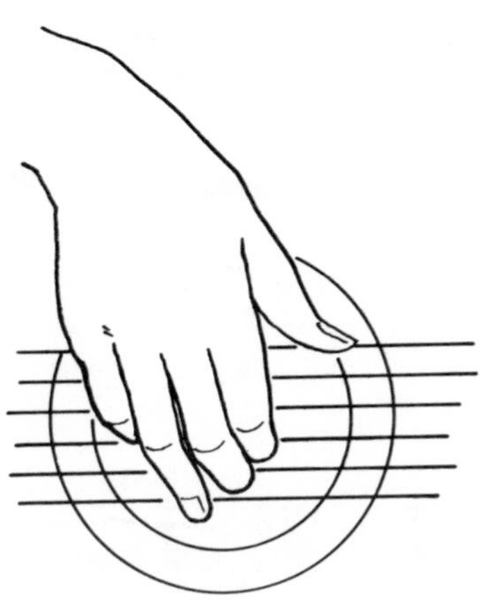

Now, slowly and evenly, pluck—first the thumb on the sixth string downward—and then the three fingers, all together, on the first three strings upward. It's not necessary to pull the strings too hard to get them to sound. Take it easy.

Try the same thing on a G chord. Don't bend your right thumb.

Try A7. Here the thumb plucks the fifth string and the fingers remain on the first three strings. Don't bend your thumb.

With D—where the thumb plucks the fourth string—it is very important that the thumb not bend, but, rather, remain stiff and circle upward away from the three fingers.

E minor is such a nice-sounding chord—let's try a song that begins with it.

When Johnny Comes Marching Home

Em
Get ready for the Jubilee,
G
Hurrah, hurrah!
Em
We'll give the hero three times three,
G
Hurrah, hurrah!
Em   D
The laurel wreath is ready now
Em   D
To place upon his loyal brow,
Em   D   Em
And we'll all feel gay when Johnny comes marching home.

Em
The old church bell will peal with joy,
G
Hurrah, hurrah!
Em
To welcome home our darling boy,
G
Hurrah, hurrah!
Em   D
The village lads and lassies say,
Em   D
With roses they will strew the way,
Em   D   Em
And we'll all feel gay when Johnny comes marching home.

Em
Let love and friendship on that day,
G
Hurrah, hurrah!
Em
Their choicest treasures then display,
G
Hurrah, hurrah!
Em   D
And let each one perform some part,
Em   D
To fill with joy the warrior's heart,
Em   D   Em
And we'll all feel gay when Johnny comes marching home.

The Key of A Major

Another set of chords (key) that go together as did D, G, and A7 is A, D, and E7. (From now on play all chords with this thumb and finger-pluck method.)

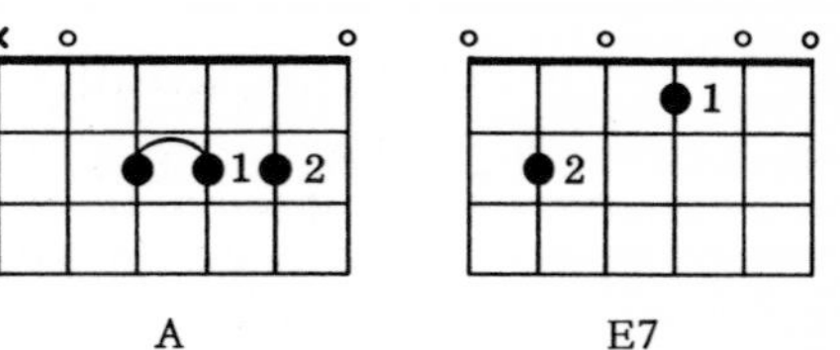

A
E7

Jacob's Ladder

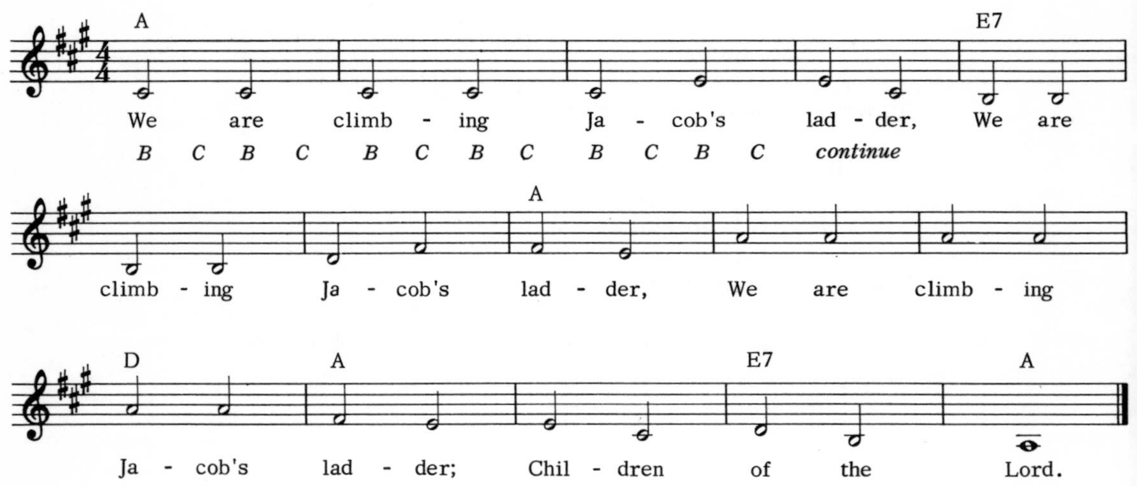

A E7
We are climb - ing Ja - cob's lad - der, We are
B C B C B C B C B C B C continue
A
climb - ing Ja - cob's lad - der, We are climb - ing
D A E7 A
Ja - cob's lad - der; Chil - dren of the Lord.

A
Every rung goes higher and higher,
E7 A
Every rung goes higher and higher,
D A
Every rung goes higher and higher,
E7 A
Children of the Lord.

A
Every new man makes us stronger,
E7 A
Every new man makes us stronger,
D A
Every new man makes us stronger,
E7 A
Children of the Lord.

A
We have toiled in dark and danger,
E7 A
We have toiled in dark and danger,
D A
We have toiled in dark and danger,
E7 A
Children of the Lord. *Repeat Verse One*

Here is a livelier version of the same spiritual.

Rise and Shine

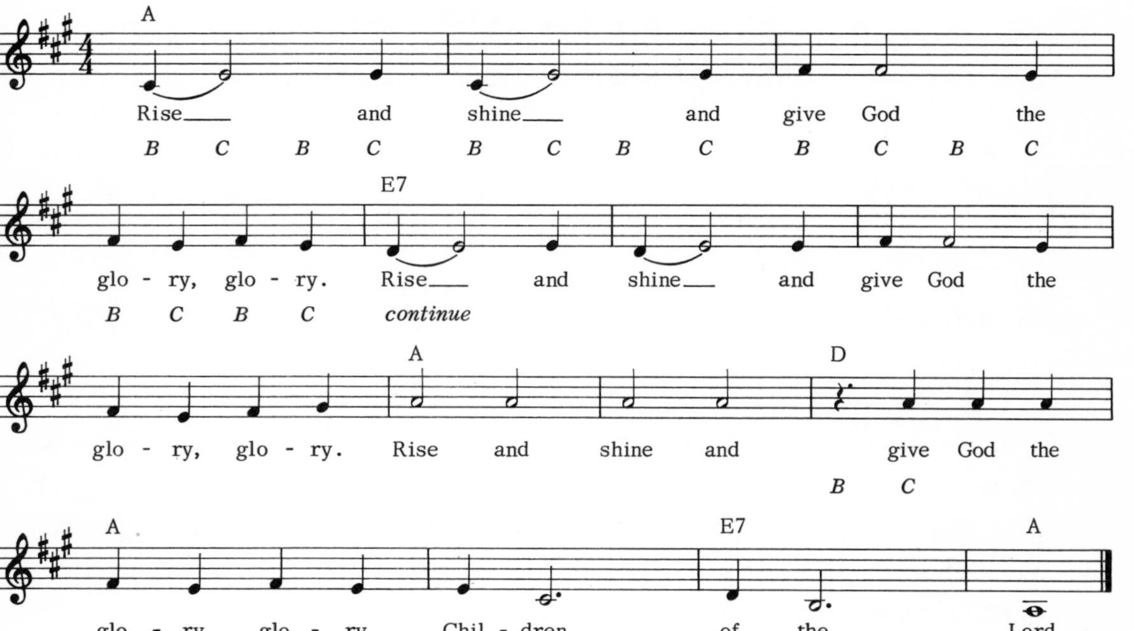

A
The Lord said, "Noah, there's gonna be a floody, floody."
E7
The Lord said, "Noah, there's gonna be a floody, floody.
A D A
Get your children out of the muddy, muddy!"
E7 A
Children of the Lord.

A
Noah, he built him, he built him an arky, arky,
E7
Noah, he built him, he built him an arky, arky.
A D A
Made it out of hickory barky, barky,
E7 A
Children of the Lord.

A
The animals, they came, they came by twosy, twosy,
E7
The animals, they came, they came by twosy, twosy,
A D A
Elephants and kangaroosy, roosy.
E7 A
Children of the Lord.

A
It rained and rained for forty daysy, daysy,
E7
It rained and rained for forty daysy, daysy,
A D A
Drove those animals nearly crazy, crazy.
E7 A
Children of the Lord. *Repeat Verse One*

Alternate Bass

The thumb need not always play one and the same string for each chord. There are usually alternate bass notes which may be played. These alternate bass notes add another element of variety to your playing.

The alternate bass for the A chord is the E (sixth) string (and the D string.)

The alternate bass for the D chord is the A string.

The alternate bass for the E7 chord is the A string.

Play the following song using alternate basses.

Camptown Races

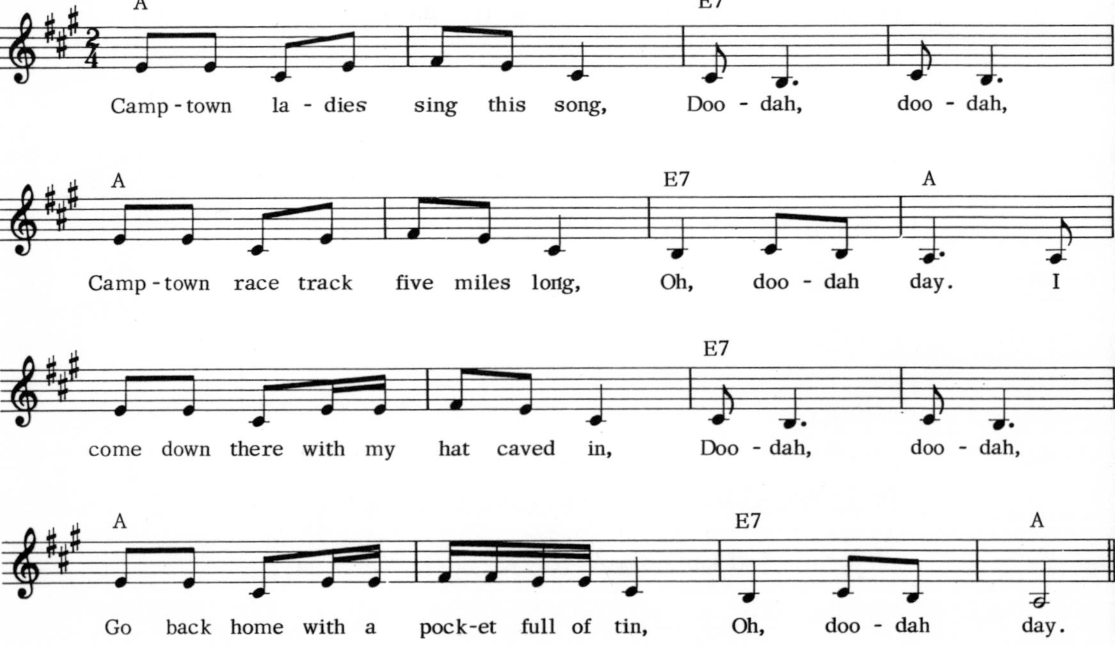
A
E7
Camp - town la - dies sing this song, Doo - dah, doo - dah,
A
E7
A
Camp - town race track five miles long, Oh, doo - dah day. I
E7
come down there with my hat caved in, Doo - dah, doo - dah,
A
E7
A
Go back home with a pock-et full of tin, Oh, doo - dah day.

Chorus

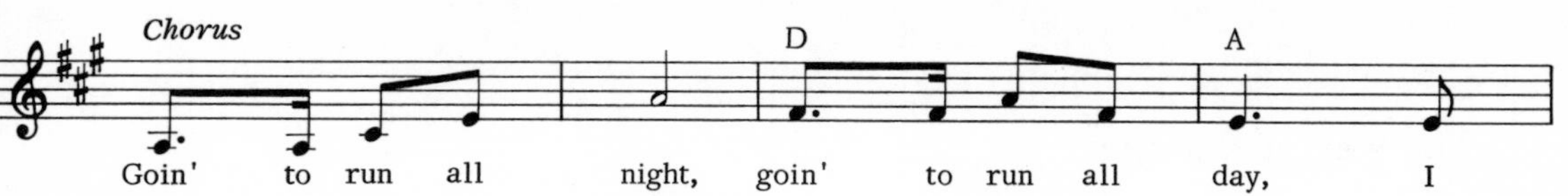
D
A
Goin' to run all night, goin' to run all day, I

E7
A
bet my mon-ey on the bob - tail nag, Some - bo - dy bet on the bay.

A
The long-tail filly and the big black hoss,
E7
Doo-dah, doo-dah,
A
They fly the track and they both cut across,
E7 A
Oh, doo-dah day.

The blind hoss sticken in a big mud hole,
E7
Doo-dah, doo-dah,
A
Can't touch bottom with a ten-foot pole,
E7 A
Oh, doo-dah day. *Chorus*

A
Old muley cow come onto the track,
E7
Doo-dah, doo-dah,
A
The bobtail fling her over his back,
E7 A
Oh, doo-dah day.

Then fly along like a railroad car,
E7
Doo-dah, doo-dah,
A
Running a race with a shooting star,
E7 A
Oh, doo-dah day. *Chorus*

A
See them flying on a ten-mile heat,
E7
Doo-dah, doo-dah,
A
'Round the race track, then repeat,
E7 A
Oh, doo-dah day.

I win my money on the bobtail nag,
E7
Doo-dah, doo-dah,
A
I keep my money in an old towbag,
E7 A
Oh, doo-dah day. *Chorus*

Review your previous songs using the thumb and finger-pluck and the alternate bass.

The alternate bass for the G chord is the A string (and the D string).

The alternate bass for the A7 chord is the E (sixth) string (and the D string.)

The alternate bass for E minor is the A string (and the D string).

The Key of E Major

The three main chords in the key of E are E, A and B7.

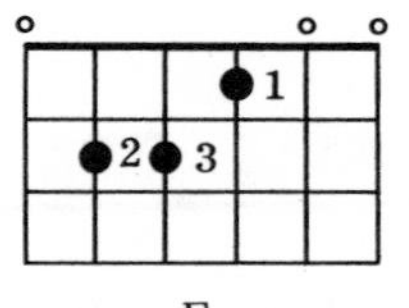

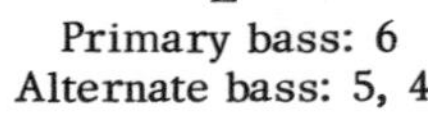

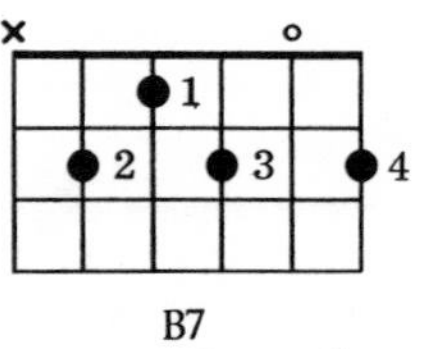

1
2
3

E
Primary bass: 6
Alternate bass: 5, 4

1
2
3
4

B7
Primary bass: 5
Alternate bass: 4

This is a traditional Shaker song.

Simple Gifts

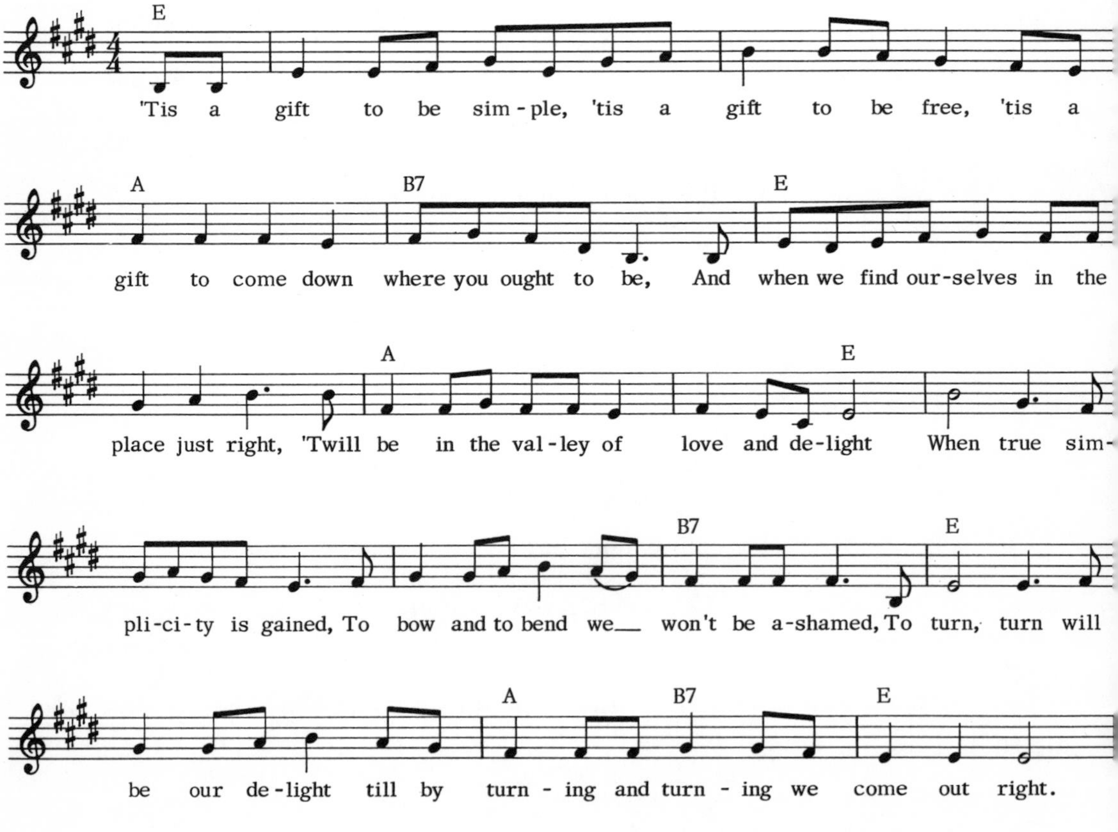

E
'Tis a gift to be sim - ple, 'tis a gift to be free, 'tis a
A B7 E
gift to come down where you ought to be, And when we find our-selves in the
A E
place just right, 'Twill be in the val - ley of love and de-light When true sim-
B7 E
pli-ci-ty is gained, To bow and to bend we__ won't be a-shamed, To turn, turn will
A B7 E
be our de-light till by turn - ing and turn - ing we come out right.

A rousing Negro spiritual.

Oh, Mary, Don't You Weep

Chorus
E B7
Oh, Mar - y, don't you weep, don't you mourn, Oh, Mar - y, don't you
E A E
weep, don't you mourn. Phar - aoh's ar - my got drown - ded
B7 E
Oh, Mar - y, don't you weep.
Verse
E
If I could I
B7 E
sure - ly would stand on the rock where Mo - ses stood.

A E B7 E
Phar - aoh's ar - my got drown - ded. Oh, Mar - y, don't you weep.

E B7
Moses stood on the Red Sea shore,
E
Smitin' that water with a two-by-four.
A E
Pharaoh's army got drownded,
B7 E
Oh, Mary, don't you weep. *Chorus*

E B7
One of these nights, about twelve o'clock,
E
This old world's gonna reel and rock.
A E
Pharaoh's army got drownded,
B7 E
Oh, Mary, don't you weep. *Chorus*

E B7
God gave Noah the rainbow sign,
E
"No more water, but fire next time!"
A E
Pharaoh's army got drownded,
B7 E
Oh, Mary, don't you weep. *Chorus*

E B7
I may be right and I may be wrong,
E
I know you're gonna miss me when I'm gone.
A E
Pharaoh's army got drownded,
B7 E
Oh, Mary, don't you weep. *Chorus*

Another spiritual freedom song.

I'm on My Way

E
B7
I'm on my way and I won't turn back,
I'm on my way and I won't turn back,
E
A
I'm on my way and I won't turn back,
E
B7
E
I'm on my way, great God, I'm on my way.

E B7
I asked my brother to come with me,
E
I asked my brother to come with me,
A
I asked my brother to come with me,
E B7 E
I'm on my way, great God, I'm on my way.

E B7
If he won't come, I'll go alone,
E
If he won't come, I'll go alone,
A
If he won't come, I'll go alone,
E B7 E
I'm on my way, great God, I'm on my way.

E B7
I asked my sister to come with me,
E
I asked my sister to come with me,
A
I asked my sister to come with me,
E B7 E
I'm on my way, great God, I'm on my way.

E B7
If she won't come, I'll go alone,
E
If she won't come, I'll go alone,
A
If she won't come, I'll go alone,
E B7 E
I'm on my way, great God, I'm on my way.

E B7
I asked my boss to let me go,
E
I asked my boss to let me go,
A
I asked my boss to let me go,
E B7 E
I'm on my way, great God, I'm on my way.

E B7
If he says, "No," I'll go anyhow,
E
If he says, "No," I'll go anyhow,
A
If he says, "No," I'll go anyhow,
E B7 E
I'm on my way, great God, I'm on my way.

E B7
I'm on my way to Freedom Land,
E
I'm on my way to Freedom Land,
A
I'm on my way to Freedom Land,
E B7 E
I'm on my way, great God, I'm on my way.

Repeat Verse One

From the chain gang.

Take This Hammer

E
B7
Take this ham - mer, car-ry it to the cap - tain,
Take this ham - mer, car-ry it to the cap - tain,
E
Take this ham - mer, car-ry it to the cap - tain,
A
Tell him I'm a - gone
E
B7
Tell him I'm a - gone
E

E B7
If he asks you, was I laughin',
E
If he asks you, was I laughin',
A
If he asks you, was I laughin',
E B7 E
Tell him I was cryin', tell him I was cryin'.

E B7
If he asks you, was I runnin',
E
If he asks you, was I runnin',
A
If he asks you, was I runnin',
E B7 E
Tell him I was flyin', tell him I was flyin'.

E B7
I don't want no cornbread and molasses,
E
I don't want no cornbread and molasses,
A
I don't want no cornbread and molasses,
E B7 E
They hurt my pride, they hurt my pride.

E B7
I don't want no cold iron shackles,
E
I don't want no cold iron shackles,
A
I don't want no cold iron shackles
E B7 E
Around my leg, around my leg.

Repeat Verse One

The Key of G Major

The three main chords
in the key of G are G, C, and D7.

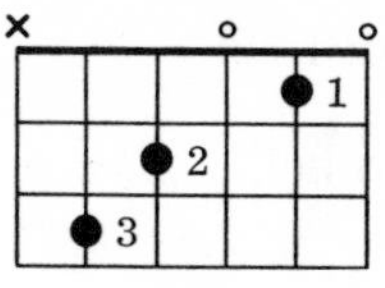

C
Primary bass: 5
Alternate bass: 4

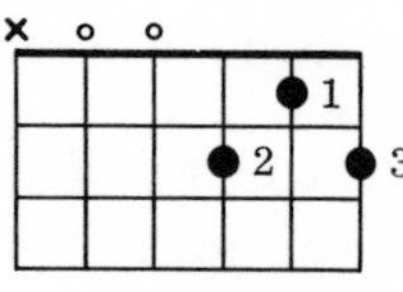

D7
Primary bass: 4
Alternate bass: 5

Little Brown Jug

G C D7 G
My wife and I lived all a - lone in a lit - tle brown jug we called our home.

C D7 G
She loved whis - key, I loved rum, I tell you what, we'd lots of fun.

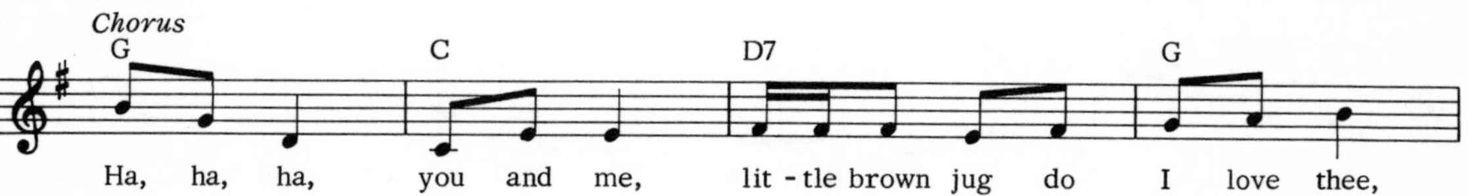
Chorus
G C D7 G
Ha, ha, ha, you and me, lit - tle brown jug do I love thee,

C D7 G
Ha, ha, ha, you and me, lit - tle brown jug do I love thee.

G C
'Tis you that makes my friends my foes,
D7 G
'Tis you that makes me wear old clothes,
C
But here you are so near my nose,
D7 G
So tip her up and down she goes. *Chorus*

G C
When I go toiling on my farm,
D7 G
Little brown jug beneath my arm.
C
Set her near some shady tree—
D7 G
Little brown jug, don't I love thee? *Chorus*

G C
I lay in the shade of a tree,
D7 G
Little brown jug in the shade of me.
C
I raised her up and gave a pull—
D7 G
Little brown jug was about half full. *Chorus*

G C
Crossed the creek on a hollow log,
D7 G
Me and the wife and the little brown dog.
C
The wife and the dog fell into the bog,
D7 G
But I held on to the little brown jug. *Chorus*

G C
One day when I went out to my farm,
D7 G
Little brown jug was under my arm,
C
Stubbed my toe and down I fell—
D7 G
Broke that little jug all to hell. *Chorus*

G C
When I die, don't bury me at all,
D7 G
Just pickle my bones in alcohol.
C
Put a bottle of booze at my head and feet,
D7 G
And then I know that I will keep. *Chorus*

A song from the American Revolution.

The Rifle

G D7 G D7 G
Why come ye hith - er, Red-coats? Your minds,what mad-ness fills? There is
D7 G D7 G D7 G
dan - ger in our val - ley and there's dan - ger in our hills, Oh
C G
hear ye not the sing - ing of the bu - gle, wild and free? Full
D7 G Chorus
soon you'll hear the ring - ing of the ri - fle from each tree. For the
C G
ri - fle, Oh, the ri - fle, In our
D7 G 1. 2.
hands will prove no tri - fle. Oh, the

G D7 G D7 G
Ye ride a goodly steed, ye may know another master,
D7 G D7 G D7 G
Ye forward come with speed, but ye'll learn to back much faster
C G
When you meet our mountain boys and their leader Johnny Stark—
D7 G
Lads who make but little noise, lads who always hit the mark. *Chorus*

G D7 G D7 G
Had ye no graves at home, across the briny water,
D7 G D7 G D7 G
That hither ye must come, like bullocks to the slaughter?
C G
Well, if we the work must do, why, the sooner 'tis begun,
D7 G
If flint and powder hold but true, the sooner 'twill be done. *Chorus*

$\frac{3}{4}$ Three-Quarter Time

The meter of all the songs we have had up to now has been either $\frac{2}{4}$ or $\frac{4}{4}$. The basic feeling of all the songs has been "one-two . . ." This is called *duple* meter. In triple meter, or three-quarter time, the basic feeling is "one-two-three . . ." In three-quarter time "one" gets the heavier accent (*thumb beat*) and "two" and "three" are each plucked upward with the fingers in the same basic movement as before.

As in duple meter, care must be taken to start singing on the correct beat of the strum. Here, too, this will vary from song to song and from stanza to stanza.

My Bonny Lies Over the Ocean

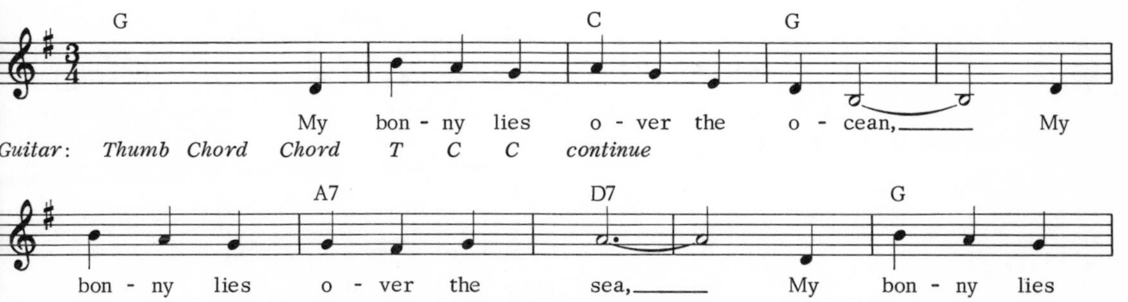

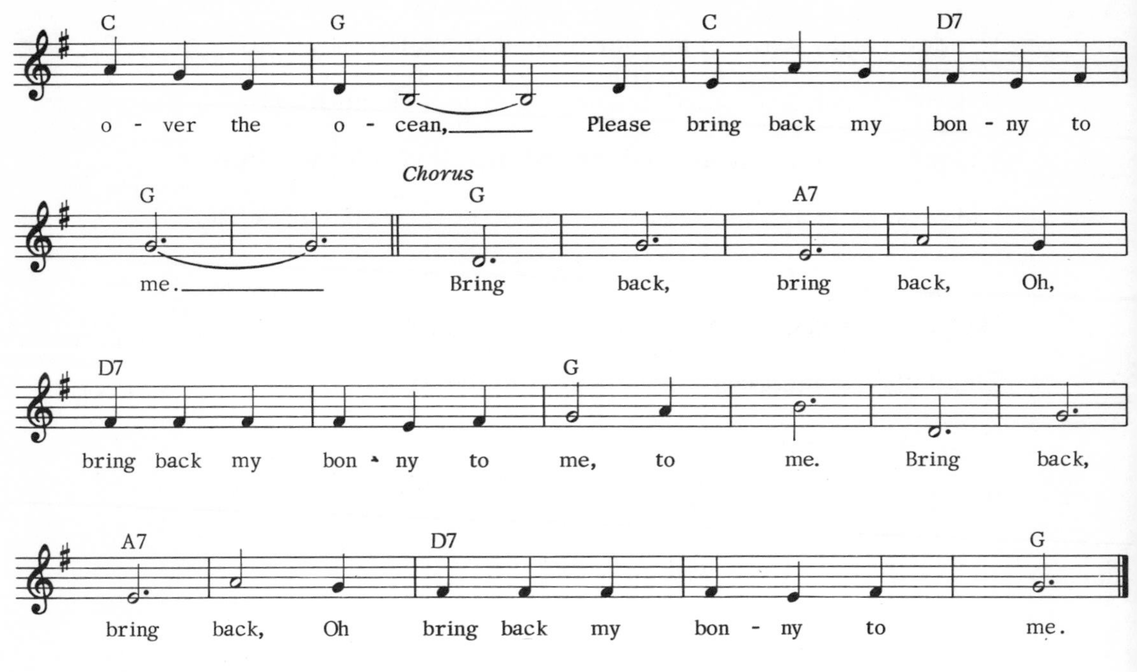
C G C D7
o - ver the o - cean, Please bring back my bon - ny to
G
me.
Chorus
G A7
Bring back, bring back, Oh,
D7 G
bring back my bon - ny to me, to me. Bring back,
A7 D7 G
bring back, Oh bring back my bon - ny to me.

G C G
Oh, blow, ye winds over the ocean,
A7 D7
And blow, ye winds over the sea.
G C G
Oh, blow, ye winds over the ocean,
C D7 G
And bring back my bonny to me. *Chorus*

G C G
Last night as I lay on my pillow,
A7 D7
Last night as I lay on my bed,
G C G
Last night as I lay on my pillow,
C D7 G
I dreamed that my bonny was dead. *Chorus*

G C G
The winds have blown over the ocean,
A7 D7
The winds have blown over the sea,
G C G
The winds have blown over the ocean,
C D7 G
And brought back my bonny to me. *Chorus*

Home on the Range

G C
Oh, give me a home, where the buf - fa - lo roam, Where the
T C C T C C continue
G A7 D7
deer and the an - te - lope play, Where

G C
sel - dom is heard a dis - cour - ag - ing word, And the
G D7 G
skies are not cloud - y all day.
Chorus
G D7 G
Home, home on the range, Where the
Em A7 D7
deer and the an - te - lope play, Where
G C
sel - dom is heard a dis - cour - ag - ing word, And the
G D7 G
skies are not cloud - y all day.

G C
How often at night when the heavens are bright
G A7 D7
With the light from the glittering stars,
G C
Have I stood there amazed and asked as I gazed,
G D7 G
If their glory exceeds that of ours. *Chorus*

G C
Where the air is so pure, the zephyrs so free,
G A7 D7
The breezes so balmy and light,
G C
That I would not exchange my home on the range
G D7 G
For all of the cities so bright. *Chorus*

G C
Oh, I love those wild flow'rs in this dear land of ours,
G A7 D7
The curlew, I love to hear scream,
G C
And I love the white rocks and the antelope flocks,
G D7 G
That graze on the mountaintops green. *Chorus*

The Key of C Major

The three main chords in the key of C are C, F, and G7.

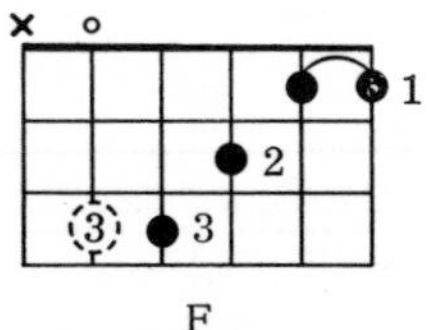

1
2
3
3

F
Primary bass: 4
Alternate bass: 5
(open or fingered)

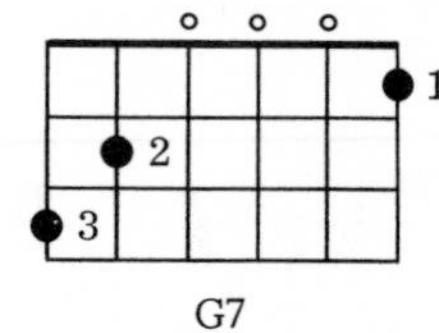

1
2
3

G7
Primary bass: 6
Alternate bass: 5, 4

Sail Away, Ladies

C G7 C G7 C
If ev-er I get my new house done, Sail a-way, la-dies, sail a-way. I'll
G7 C G7 C
give my old one to my son, Sail a-way, la-dies, sail a-way.
Chorus
C F C
Don't she rock 'em, die - di - o, Don't she rock 'em, die - di - o,
G7 C
Don't she rock 'em, die - di - o, Don't she rock 'em, die - di - o.

C G7 C
Children, don't you grieve and cry,
G7 C
Sail away, ladies, sail away,
G7 C
You're gonna be angels by and by.
G7 C
Sail away, ladies, sail away. *Chorus*

C G7 C
Come along, girls, and go with me,
G7 C
Sail away, ladies, sail away,
G7 C
We'll go back to Tennessee.
G7 C
Sail away, ladies, sail away. *Chorus*

C G7 C
I got a letter from Shiloh town,
G7 C
Sail away, ladies, sail away,
G7 C
Big Saint Louie is a-burning down,
G7 C
Sail away, ladies, sail away. *Chorus*

C G7 C
I chew my tobacco and I spit my juice,
G7 C
Sail away, ladies, sail away,
G7 C
I love my own daughter but it ain't no use,
G7 C
Sail away, ladies, sail away. *Chorus*

In this old Negro spiritual the words "kum ba ya" probably are derived from "come by here."

Kum Ba Ya

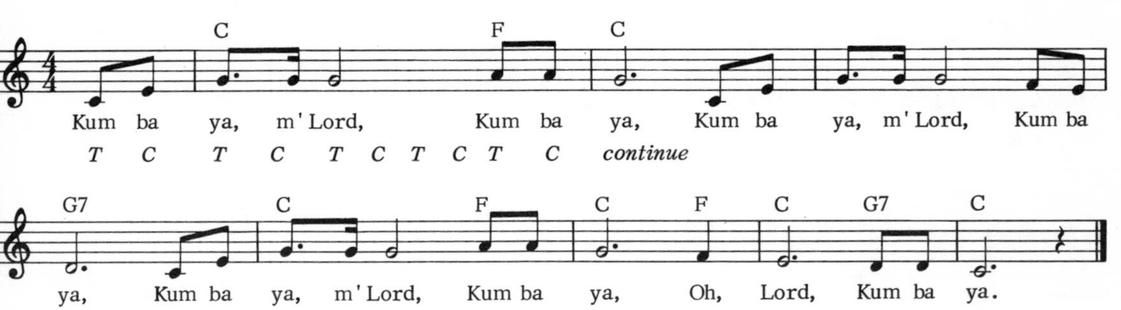

C F C
Someone's singing, Lord, kum ba ya,
G7
Someone's singing, Lord, kum ba ya,
C F C
Someone's singing, Lord, kum ba ya,
F C G7 C
Oh, Lord, kum ba ya.

C F C
Someone's dancing, Lord, kum ba ya,
G7
Someone's dancing, Lord, kum ba ya,
C F C
Someone's dancing, Lord, kum ba ya,
F C G7 C
Oh, Lord, kum ba ya.

C F C
Someone's weeping, Lord, kum ba ya,
G7
Someone's weeping, Lord, kum ba ya,
C F C
Someone's weeping, Lord, kum ba ya,
F C G7 C
Oh, Lord, kum ba ya.

C F C
Someone's shouting, Lord, kum ba ya,
G7
Someone's shouting, Lord, kum ba ya,
C F C
Someone's shouting, Lord, kum ba ya
F C G7 C
Oh, Lord, kum ba ya.

C F C
Someone's praying, Lord, kum ba ya,
G7
Someone's praying, Lord, kum ba ya,
C F C
Someone's praying, Lord, kum ba ya,
F C G7 C
Oh, Lord, kum ba ya.

A cowboy song in $\frac{3}{4}$ time.

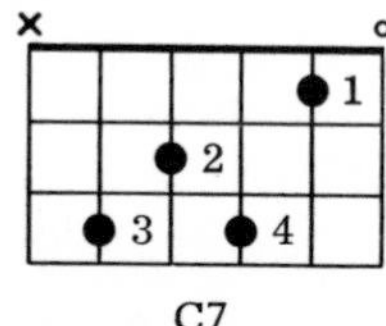

C7
Primary bass: 5
Alternate bass: 4

Git Along, Little Dogies

C F G7 C
As I was a walk - in' one morn - ing for pleas - ure, I
T C C T C C continue

F G7 C
spied a cow - punch - er a stroll - in' a - long. His

F G7 C
hat was throwed back and his spurs were a - jing - lin', And

F G7 C
as he ap - proached he was sing - ing this song.

Chorus

C7 F
Whoop-ee ti - yi - yo, Git a - long lit - tle do - gies, It's

C7 F
your____ mis - for - tune, and none of my own, Whoop - ee

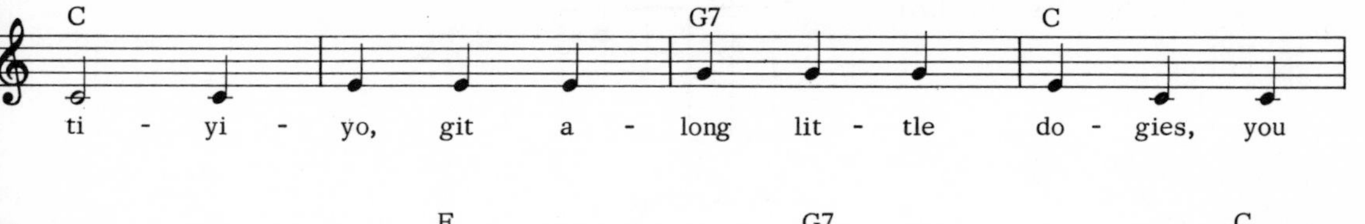
C G7 C
ti - yi - yo, git a - long lit - tle do - gies, you

F G7 C
know that Wy - o - ming will be your new home.

C F G7 C
It's early in the spring that we round up the dogies,
F G7 C
We mark them and brand them and bob off their tails;
F G7 C
We round up the horses, load up the chuck wagon,
F G7 C
And then throw the dogies upon the long trail. *Chorus*

C F G7 C
Your mother was raised away down in Texas,
F G7 C
Where the jimpson weed and the sand-burrs grow,
F G7 C
Now we'll fill you up on prickly pear and cactus,
F G7 C
Till you are all ready for the trail to Idaho. *Chorus*

C F G7 C
Oh, you'll be soup for Uncle Sam's soldiers,
F G7 C
It's, "Beef, more beef," I hear them cry.
F G7 C
Git along, git along, git along little dogies,
F G7 C
You'll be beef steers by and by. *Chorus*

An old Scottish ballad.

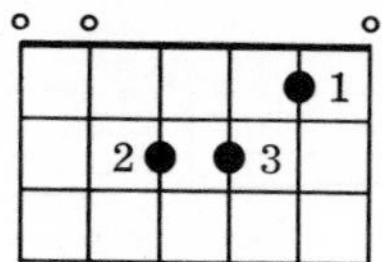

A minor
Primary bass: 5
Alternate bass: 6, 4

Tam Pierce

C G7 C

Tam Pierce, Tam Pierce, lend me your gray mare. All a-long,

T C C T C C continue

D7 G7 C

down a-long, out a-long lea, For I want for to

G7 Am *Chorus*

go ___ to Wid-de-comb Fair, With Bill Brew-er, Jan

Stew-er, Pet-er Guer-ney, Pet-er Da-vy, Dan-'l

G7

Whid-don, Har-ry Hawk, Old Un-cle Tom Cob-leigh and

C G7 C G7 C

all, ___ Old Un-cle Tom Cob-leigh and all. ___

C G7 C
And when shall I see again my gray mare?

D7 G7
All along, down along, out along, lea.

C G7 Am
By Friday soon or Saturday noon. *Chorus*

C G7 C
Then Friday came, and Saturday noon,
D7 G7
All along, down along, out along, lea,
C G7 Am
But Tam Pierce's old mare had not trotted home. *Chorus*

C G7 C
So Tam Pierce he got to the top of the hill,
D7 G7
All along, down along, out along, lea,
C G7 Am
And he seed his old mare down a-making her will. *Chorus*

C G7 C
So Tam Pierce's old mare, her took sick and died,
D7 G7
All along, down along, out along, lea,
C G7 Am
And Tam he sat down on a stone and he cried. *Chorus*

C G7 C
But this isn't the end o' this shocking affair,
D7 G7
All along, down along, out along, lea.
C G7 Am
Nor, though they be dead, of the horrid career of Bill . . . *Chorus*

C G7 C
When the wind whistles cold on the moor of a night,
D7 G7
All along, down along, out along, lea,
C G7 Am
Tam Pierce's old mare doth appear ghastly white. *Chorus*

C G7 C
And all night long be heard skirling and groans,
D7 G7
All along, down along, out along, lea,
C G7 Am
From Tam Pierce's old mare in her rattling bones. *Chorus*

This concludes the first section of this book, which has been devoted to the learning of basic chords in five keys (C,G,D,A,E) and the fundamental *thumb and finger-pluck* and the *right-hand strum.*

SECTION TWO

ARPEGGIOS

Arpeggios in Four-Quarter Time

The characteristically beautiful sound of the guitar begins to be heard when individual notes of chords are played in some pattern. These patterns are generally referred to as *arpeggios*. The word, itself, comes from the Italian, *arpa* (harp).

Finger a C chord.

Pluck the A string with the thumb—followed by the first, second and third fingers plucking their respective strings one after the other. All four notes should be played at the same speed—slowly and evenly.

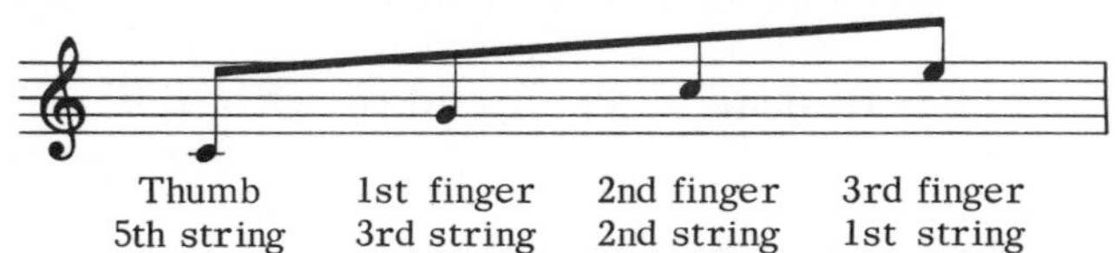

Try it on some other chords. E minor is a good one because of its open strings.

Now try F. Do all the notes sound clearly?

Here is a new chord.

Try the arpeggios with D minor.

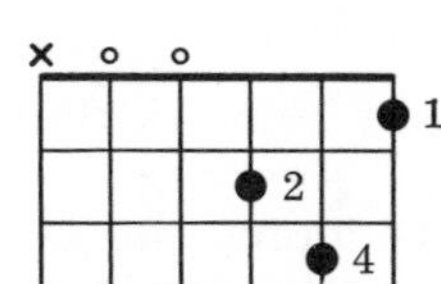

D minor
Primary bass: 4
Alternate bass: 5

This song comes to us from Pennsylvania.

When I First Came to This Land

C Em F C G7
When I first came to this land, I was
Guitar:
T 1 2 3 T 1 2 3 continue
C G7 C Em F
not a wealth - y man, so I got my - self a
C Dm G7 C Dm
1. shack, I did what I could. And I
2. cow,
3. duck,
4. wife,
5. son,
G7 C G7 Am C
called my 1. shack, "Break my back" But the land was
2. cow, "No milk now"
3. duck, "Out of luck"
4. wife, "Run for your life"
5. son, "My work's done"

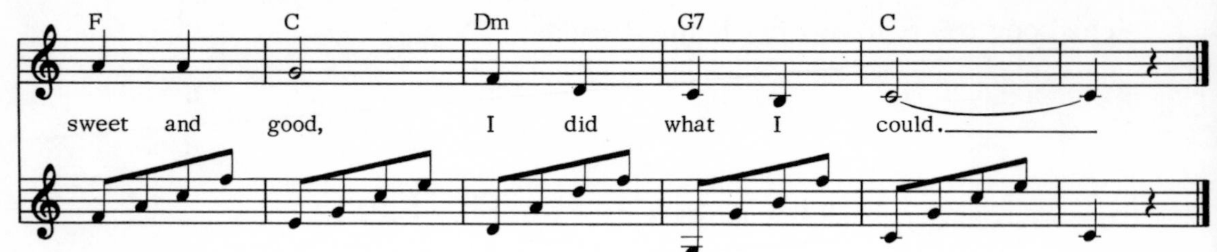

Add verses cumulatively starting from the beginning of the song each time. For example, when you get to verse 5 you should be singing

C Em F C
. . . So I got myself a son,
Dm G7 C
I did what I could.
G7 C G7 Am
And I called my son, "My work's done,"
G7 C G7 Am
And I called my wife, "Run for your life,"
G7 C G7 Am
And I called my duck, "Out of luck,"
G7 C G7 Am
And I called my cow, "No milk now,"
G7 C G7 Am
And I called my shack, "Break my back."
C F C
But the land was sweet and good,
Dm G7 C
I did what I could.

Try this arpeggio pattern.

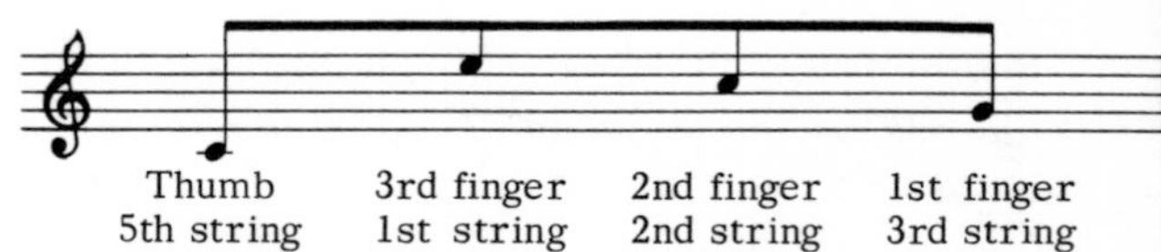

Aura Lee

G
C
tree
Sat and piped I heard him sing,
D7
G
Sing of Au - ra Lee.
Au - ra Lee,
G augmented(+)
C
C minor
Au - ra Lee,
Maid of gold - en
G
E7
A7
hair,
Sun - shine came a - long with thee, And
D7
G
swal - lows in the air.

G   C
In thy blush the rose was born;
D7   G
Music when you spake.
                        C
Through thine azure eyes the moon
D7   G
Sparkling seemed to break.
           G+
    Aura Lee, Aura Lee,
    C   Cm   G
    Birds of crimson wing
         E7   A7
    Never song have sung to me
       D7   G
    As in that bright, sweet spring.

G   C
Aura Lee, the bird may flee,
      D7   G
The willow's golden hair
                          C
Swing through winter fitfully,
D7   G
On the stormy air.
                 G+
    Yet if thy blue eyes I see,
    C   Cm   G
    Gloom will soon depart.
           E7   A7
    For to me, sweet Aura Lee
       D7   G
    Is sunshine through the heart.

G   C
When the mistletoe was green,
 D7   G
'Midst the winter's snows,
                 C
Sunshine in thy face was seen,
D7   G
Kissing lips of rose.
           G+
    Aura Lee, Aura Lee,
    C   Cm   G
    Take my golden ring.
              E7   A7
    Love and light return with thee,
         D7   G
    And swallows with the spring.

For faster-moving folksongs we often play a strum involving the alternation between "bass-chord" and arpeggios. Usually the "one-two" of the "bass-chord" comes first—followed by the exactly twice-as-fast "one-and-two-and" of the arpeggio.

Hand Me Down My Walking Cane

Guitar rhythm:
continue
E
Oh, hand me down my walk-ing cane, Oh, hand me
B7 E A
down my walk-ing cane, Hand me down my walk-ing cane,
E B7 E
I'm gon-na take the morn-ing train, 'cause all my sins are tak-en a-way.

E
Oh, hand me down my bottle o' corn,
B7 E
Oh, hand me down my bottle o' corn,
A
Hand me down my bottle o' corn,
E
I'm gonna get drunk as sure as you're born,
B7 E
'Cause all my sins are taken away.

E
Oh, I got drunk and I landed in jail,
B7 E
Oh, I got drunk and I landed in jail,
A
I got drunk and I landed in jail,
E
Had nobody for to go my bail,
B7 E
'Cause all my sins are taken away.

E
Come on, Momma, and go my bail,
B7 E
Come on, Momma, and go my bail,
A
Come on, Momma, and go my bail,
E
And get me outa this goldern jail,
B7 E
'Cause all my sins are taken away.

E
Oh, the meat was tough and the beans was bad,
B7 E
Oh, the meat was tough and the beans was bad,
A
The meat was tough and the beans was bad,
E
Oh my gosh, I can't eat that,
B7 E
'Cause all my sins are taken away.

E
Oh, if I'd listened to what Momma said,
B7 E
Oh, if I'd listened to what Momma said,
A
If I'd listened to what Momma said,
E
I'd be home in a feather bed,
B7 E
'Cause all my sins are taken away.

The Titanic

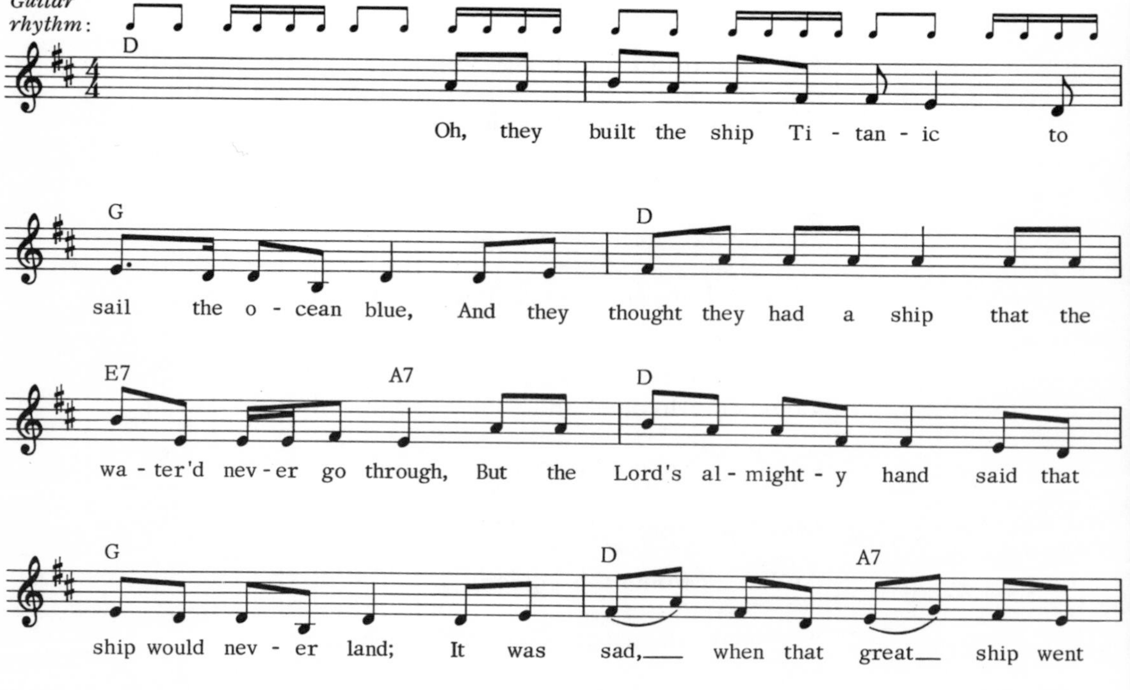

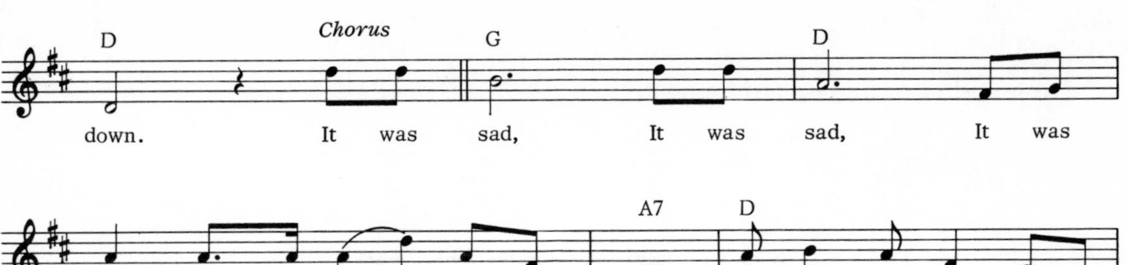
D
Chorus
G
D
down. It was sad, It was sad, It was
A7
D
sad when the great___ ship went down, Hus-bands and wives, lit - tle

G
D
A7
D
chil-dren lost their lives, It was sad___ when the great___ ship went down.

D
Oh, they sailed from England's shore
G
'Bout a thousand miles or more,
D E7 A7
When the rich refused to associate with the poor.
D
So they put them down below,
G
Where they'd be the first to go—
D A7 D
It was sad when that great ship went down. *Chorus*

D
Oh, the boat was full of sin,
G
And the sides about to burst,
D E7 A7
When the captain shouted, "Women and children first!"
D
Oh, the captain tried to wire,
G
But the lines were all on fire—
D A7 D
It was sad when that great ship went down. *Chorus*

D
Oh, they swung the lifeboats out
G
O'er the deep and raging sea,
D E7 A7
And the band struck up with "A-nearer, My God, to Thee."
D
Little children wept and cried
G
As the waves swept o'er the side—
D A7 D
It was sad when that great ship went down. *Chorus*

Arpeggios in Three-Quarter Time

Finger a C chord and play the following arpeggio pattern:

Drink to Me Only With Thine Eyes

C Dm C

Drink to me on - - ly with____ thine

F C (G bass) G7 C

eyes,____ And I____ will pledge with mine;____

Dm C

____ Or leave a kiss with - in____ the

F C (G bass) G7 C

cup____ and I'll____ not ask for wine.____

Em
The thirst that from the soul doth
Gm6 A7 D7
rise, Doth ask a drink di - vine,
G7 C Dm C7
But might I of Jove's nec - tar
Fm C (G bass) G7 C
sip, I would not ask for wine.

C Dm C F
I sent thee late a rosy wreath,
C G7 C
Not so much honoring thee,
Dm C F
As giving it a hope that there
C G7 C
It could not withered be.

Em
But thou thereon didst only breathe,
Gm6 A7 D7-G7
And send'st it back to me,
C Dm C7 Fm
Since when it grows and smells, I swear,
C G7 C
Not of itself, but thee.

Believe Me, If all Those Endearing Young Charms

C F
It is not while beauty and youth are thine own,
C G7 C G7
And thy cheeks unprofaned by a tear;
C F
But the fervor and faith of a soul can be known,
C G7 C
To which time will but make thee more dear.

F
Oh, the heart that has truly loved never forgets,
C Dm E G7
But as truly loves on to the close
C C7 F F♯dim
As the sunflower turns on her god when he sets
C G7 C
The same look that she gave when he rose.

In three-quarter time a "bass-chord-chord" strum may alternate with an arpeggio.

Blow the Man Down

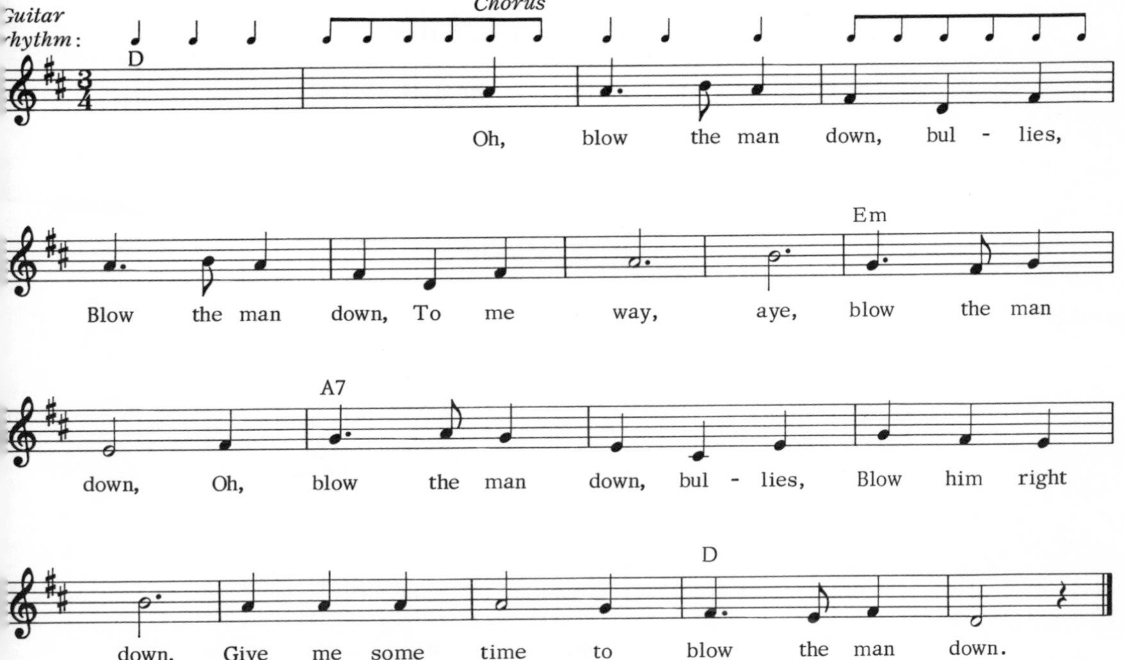

D
As I was a-walking down Paradise Street,
Em
To me way, aye, blow the man down,
A7
A pretty young damsel I chanced for to meet,
D
Give me some time to blow the man down. *Chorus*

D
She was round in the counter and bluff in the bow,
Em
To me way, aye, blow the man down,
A7
So I took in all sail and cried, "Way enough now!"
D
Give me some time to blow the man down. *Chorus*

D
I hailed her in English, she answered me clear,
Em
To me way, aye, blow the man down,
A7
"I'm from the 'Black Arrow' bound to the 'Shakespeare',"
D
Give me some time to blow the man down. *Chorus*

D
So I tailed her my flipper and took her in tow,
Em
To me way, aye, blow the man down,
A7
And yardarm to yardarm away we did go,
D
Give me some time to blow the man down. *Chorus*

D
And as we were going she said unto me,
Em
To me way, aye, blow the man down,
A7
"There's a spanking full-rigger just ready for sea."
D
Give me some time to blow the man down. *Chorus*

D
That spanking full-rigger for New York was bound,
Em
To me way, aye, blow the man down,
A7
She was very well manned and very well found,
D
Give me some time to blow the man down. *Chorus*

D
But as soon as that packet was clear of the bar,
Em
To me way, aye, blow the man down,
A7
The mate knocked me down with the end of a spar,
D
Give me some time to blow the man down. *Chorus*

D
And as soon as that packet was out on the sea,
Em
To me way, aye, blow the man down,
A7
'Twas devlish hard treatment of every degree,
D
Give me some time to blow the man down. *Chorus*

D
So I give you fair warning before we belay,
Em
To me way, aye, blow the man down,
A7
Don't never take heed of what pretty girls say,
D
Give me some time to blow the man down. *Chorus*

The Boston Come-All-Ye

uitar
ythm:
G
Come all ye young sail - or - men, lis - ten to me, I'll
C G D7 G
sing you a song of the fish of the sea.
Chorus
C G
Then blow ye winds west - er - ly, west - er - ly blow We're
D7 G
bound to the south - ward, so stead - y she goes.

G
Oh, first come the whale, the biggest of all,
C G D7 G
He clumb up aloft and let every sail fall. *Chorus*

G
And next come the mackerel with his striped back,
C G D7 G
He hauled aft the sheets and he boarded each tack. *Chorus*

G
Then come the porpoise with his short snout,
C G D7 G
He went to the wheel, calling, "Ready! About!" *Chorus*

G
Then come the smelt, the smallest of all,
C G D7 G
He jumped to the poop and sung out, "Topsail, haul!" *Chorus*

G
The herring came saying, "I'm king of the seas,
C G D7 G
"If you want any wind, I'll blow you a breeze." *Chorus*

G
Next come the cod with his chuckle-head,
C G D7 G
He went to the main-chains to heave at the lead. *Chorus*

G
Last come the flounder as flat as the ground,
C G D7 G
Says, "Damn your eyes, chuckle-head, mind how you sound." *Chorus*

$\frac{6}{8}$ Six-Eight Time

In six-eight time there are six beats per measure. Each beat is an eighth note. The six notes may be divided into three groups of two $\frac{6}{8}$

or two groups of three. $\frac{6}{8}$

It is this latter case that we will consider here.

Finger an A chord and play the following arpeggio pattern:

A
T 1 2 T 1 2
alternate bass

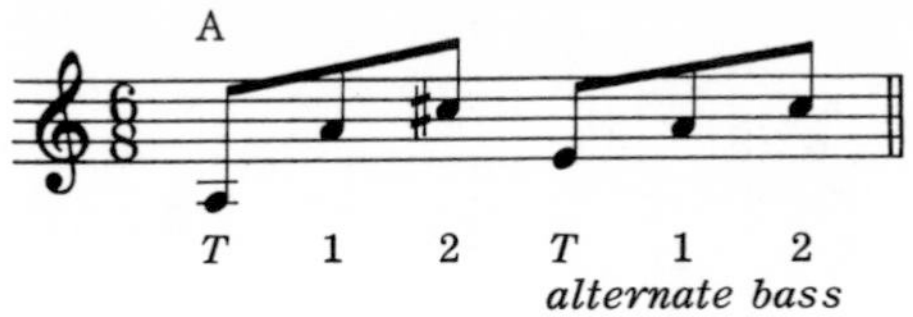

Notice that there are two main beats per measure—the first eighth and the fourth eighth.

Animal Fair

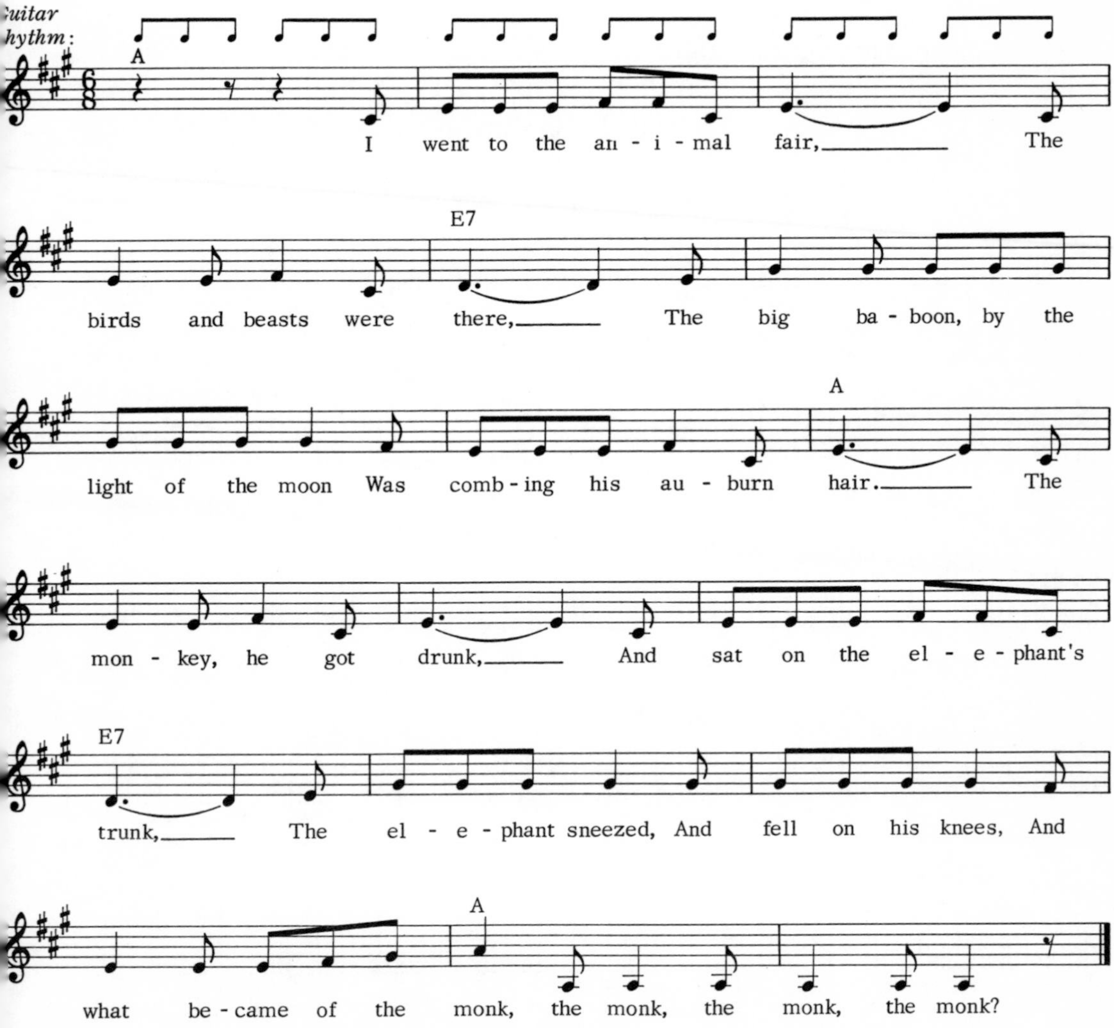

Guitar rhythm:
A
I went to the an - i - mal fair, The
E7
birds and beasts were there, The big ba - boon, by the
A
light of the moon Was comb - ing his au - burn hair. The
mon - key, he got drunk, And sat on the el - e - phant's
E7
trunk, The el - e - phant sneezed, And fell on his knees, And
A
what be - came of the monk, the monk, the monk, the monk?

There is a "base-chord-arpeggio" variation of this $\frac{6}{8}$ pattern.

Give the first thumb beat two counts and play an up pluck with the fingers on the third.

Play E minor.

Em
T chord T chord
Count: 1 - 2 3 4 - 5 6

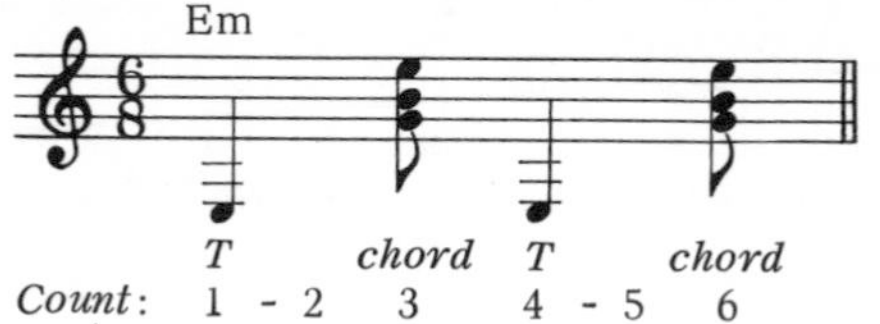

Follow this with "4, 5, 6" of the arpeggio.

T chord T 1 2
Count: 1 - 2 3 4 5 6

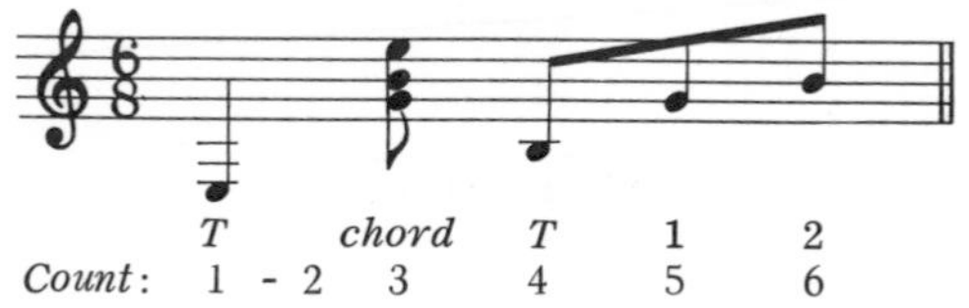

An old English pirate ballad.

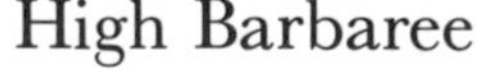

High Barbaree

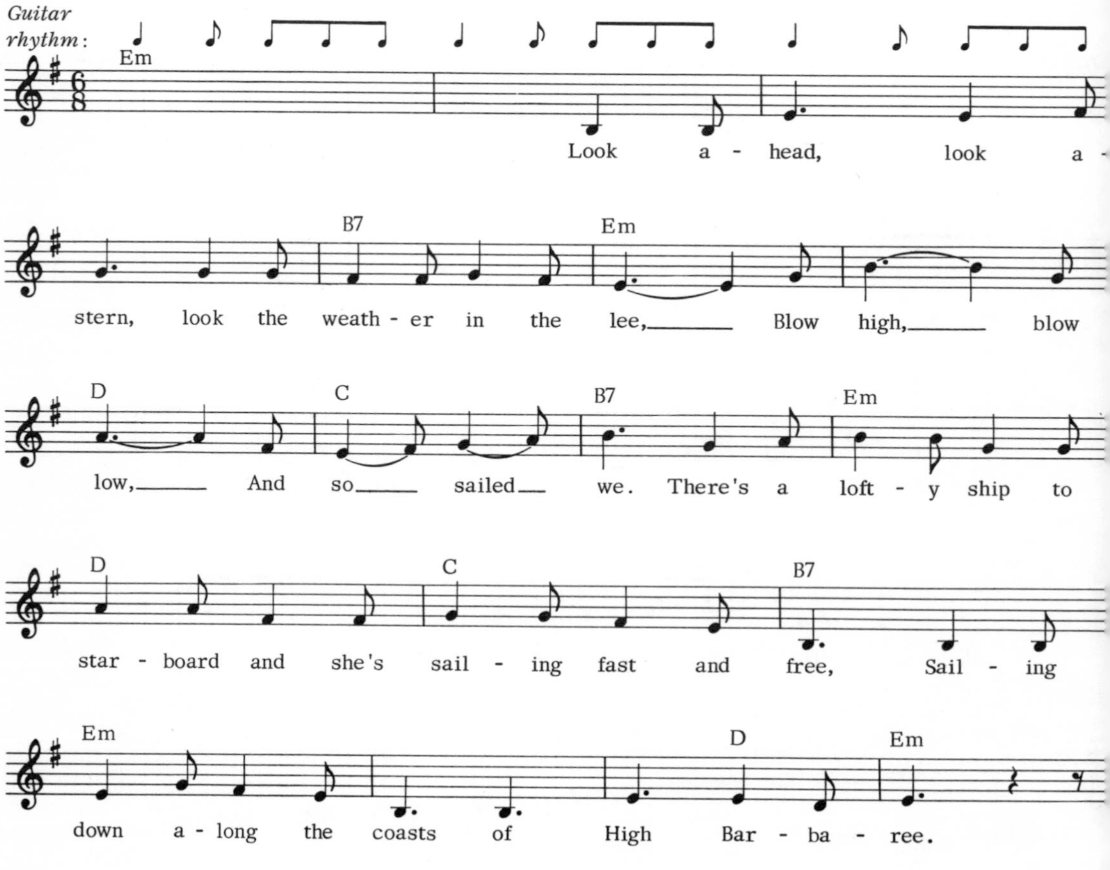

Guitar rhythm:
Em
Look a - head, look a -
B7 Em
stern, look the weath - er in the lee, Blow high, blow
D C B7 Em
low, And so sailed we. There's a loft - y ship to
D C B7
star - board and she's sail - ing fast and free, Sail - ing
Em D Em
down a - long the coasts of High Bar - ba - ree.

Em B7 Em
"Oh, are you a pirate or a man-o-war?" cried we.
D C B7
Blow high, blow low, and so sailed we.
Em D C B7
"Oh, no I'm not a pirate but a man-o-war," cried he.
Em D Em
Sailing down along the coasts of High Barbaree.

Em B7 Em
"Then back up your topsails and heave your vessel to."
D C B7
Blow high, blow low, and so sailed we.
Em D C B7
"For we have got some letters to be carried home by you."
Em D Em
Sailing down along the coasts of High Barbaree.

Em B7 Em
"We'll back up our topsail and heave our vessel to."
D C B7
Blow high, blow low, and so sailed we.
Em D C B7
"But only in some harbor and along the side of you."
Em D Em
Sailing down along the coasts of High Barbaree.

Em B7 Em
For broadside and broadside they fought all on the main.
D C B7
Blow high, blow low, and so sailed we.
Em D C B7
Until at last the frigate shot the pirate's mast away.
Em D Em
Sailing down along the coasts of High Barbaree.

Em B7 Em
For quarter, for quarter, the saucy pirates cried.
D C B7
Blow high, blow low, and so sailed we.
Em D C B7
But the quarter that we showed them was to sink them in the tide,
Em D Em
Sailing down along the coasts of High Barbaree.

Em B7 Em
With cutlass and gun, oh, we fought for hours three.
D C B7
Blow high, blow low, and so sailed we.
Em D C B7
The ship it was their coffin, and their grave it was the sea.
Em D Em
Sailing down along the coasts of High Barbaree.

One of the earliest American presidential campaign songs.

Jefferson and Liberty

Guitar rhythm:
Em D Em B7 Em Chorus G D Em D G Am B7 Em
The gloom - y night be - fore us flies, The reign of ter - ror
now is o'er Its gags, in - quis - i - tors and spies, Its
herds of harp - ies are no more, Re - joice, Co-lum - bia's sons, re-joice, to
ty - rants nev - er bend the knee, But join with heart and
soul and voice, For Jeff - er - son and li - ber - ty.

Em
No lordling here, with gorging jaws,
D
Shall wring from industry the food;
Em
Nor fiery bigot's holy laws
B7 Em
Lay waste our fields and streets in blood. *Chorus*

Em
Here strangers from a thousand shores,
D
Compelled by tyranny to roam,
Em
Shall find, amidst abundant stores,
B7 Em
A nobler and a happier home. *Chorus*

Em
Here Art shall lift her laureled head,
D
Wealth, Industry and Peace divine;
Em
And where dark pathless forests spread,
B7 Em
Rich fields and lofty cities shine. *Chorus*

An Italian folksong.

Funiculi, Funicula

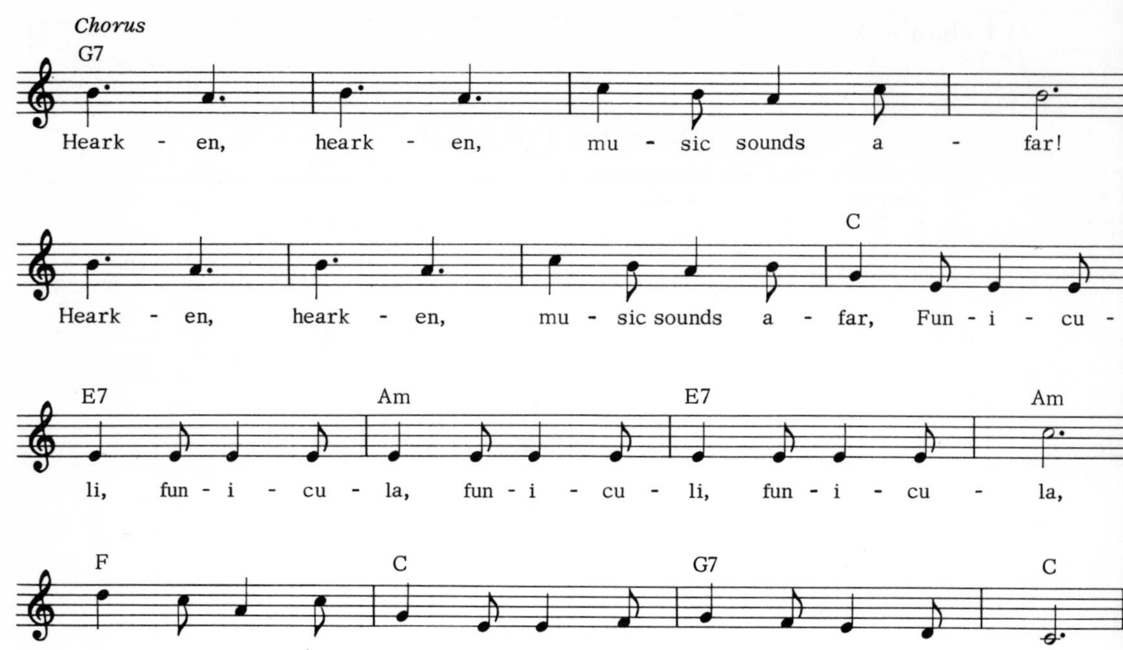
Chorus
G7
Heark - en, heark - en, mu - sic sounds a - far!
C
Heark - en, heark - en, mu - sic sounds a - far, Fun - i - cu -
E7 Am E7 Am
li, fun - i - cu - la, fun - i - cu - li, fun - i - cu - la,
F C G7 C
Joy is ev - 'ry - where, fun - i - cu - li, fun - i - cu - la.

C
Ah, me! 'Tis strange that some should take to sighing,
G7 C G7 C
And like it well, and like it well.

For me, I have not thought it worth the trying,
G7 C G7 C
So cannot tell, so cannot tell.
Em B7 Em B7 Em
With laugh, and dance, and song, the day soon passes,
B7 Em B7 Em
Full soon is gone, full soon is gone.
G D7 G D7 G
For mirth was made for joyous lads and lasses
D7 G D7 G
To call their own, to call their own! *Chorus*

Here are two old English ballads which are sometimes written in $\frac{3}{4}$ and sometimes in $\frac{6}{8}$ time. It will be easier to read them here in $\frac{3}{4}$. The arpeggio is the same as in *Drink to Me Only With Thine Eyes* and *Believe Me, If All Those Endearing Young Charms.*

Greensleeves

Em D
I have been ready at your hand
Em B7
To grant whatever you would crave;
Em D
I have both wagered life and land,
Em B7 Em
Your love and good will for to have. *Chorus*

Em D
I bought thee kerchiefs to thy head
Em B7
That were wrought fine and gallantly;
Em D
I kept thee both at board and bed,
Em B7 Em
Which cost my purse well favoredly. *Chorus*

Em D
Thy smock of gold so crimson red,
Em B7
With pearls bedeckèd sumptuously.
Em D
The like no other lasses had,
Em B7 Em
And yet thou wouldest not love me. *Chorus*

Em D
Thy gown was of the grassy green,
Em B7
Thy sleeves of satin hanging by;
Em D
Which made thee be our harvest queen,
Em B7 Em
And yet thou wouldest not love me. *Chorus*

Em D
Thou couldst desire no earthly thing,
Em B7
But still thou hadst it readily;
Em D
Thy music still to play and sing,
Em B7 Em
And yet thou wouldest not love me. *Chorus*

Em D
Well, I will pray to God on high
Em B7
That thou my constancy mayst see;
Em D
And that yet once before I die
Em B7 Em
Thou wilt vouchsafe to love me. *Chorus*

Em D
Greensleeves, now farewell, adieu!
Em B7
God I pray to prosper thee;
Em D
For I am still thy lover true—
Em B7 Em
Come once again and love me. *Chorus*

When a chord changes on the third beat of a measure, as happens throughout this next song, the arpeggio is played in the following manner: The first four notes of the arpeggio are played on the first chord and the last two (the fifth and sixth) are played on the new chord. The thumb strikes the bass note of the new chord on the fifth beat (to emphasize the chord change) simultaneously with the second finger playing the second string. The first finger completes the sequence by playing the third string as usual

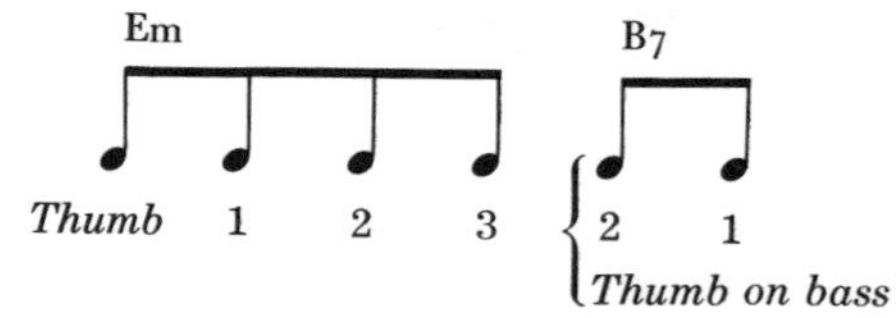

The Willow Song

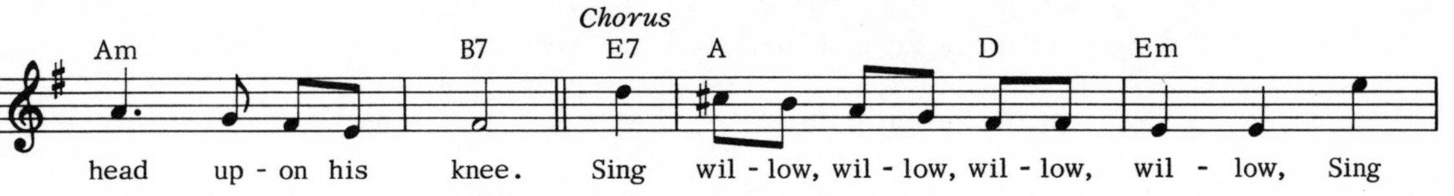
Chorus
Am B7 E7 A D Em
head up - on his knee. Sing wil - low, wil - low, wil - low, wil - low, Sing

B7 E Em B7 Em
wil - low, wil - low, wil - low, wil - low, my gar - land shall be. Sing

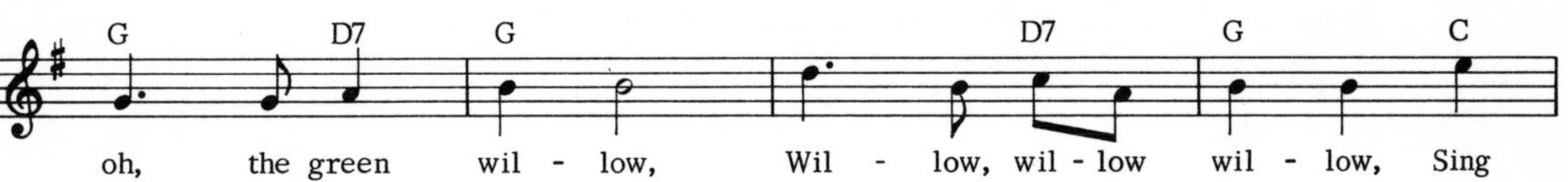
G D7 G D7 G C
oh, the green wil - low, Wil - low, wil - low wil - low, Sing

G B7 Em Am B7 Em
oh, the green wil - low my gar - land shall be.

Em B7 Em G D7 G
He sighed in his singing and made a great moan,
Em
Sing, oh, the green willow.
G D7 G Am B7
I am dead to all pleasure, my true love she is gone. *Chorus*

Em B7 Em G D7 G
The mute bird sat by him, was made tame by his moans,
Em
Sing, oh, the green willow.
G D7 G Am B7
The true tears fell from him would have melted the stones. *Chorus*

Em B7 Em G D7 G
Come all you forsaken and mourn you with me;
Em
Sing, oh, the green willow.
G D7 G Am B7
Who speaks of a false love, mine's falser than she. *Chorus*

Em B7 Em G D7 G
Let Love no more boast her in palace nor bower,
Em
Sing, oh, the green willow.
G D7 G Am B7
It buds but it blasteth, ere it be a flower. *Chorus*

```
      Em          B7      Em         G                  D7  G
Thou fair and more false, I died with thy wound,
               Em
      Sing, oh, the green willow.
               G            D7       G              Am                  B7
Thou hast lost the truest lover that goes upon the ground.   Chorus

    Em     B7 Em                 G           D7       G
Let nobody chide her, her frowns I approve,
               Em
      Sing, oh, the green willow.
           G            D7 G             Am            B7
She was born to be false and I to die of love.   Chorus

     Em        B7   Em                 G          D7 G
Take this for my farewell and latest adieu,
               Em
      Sing, oh, the green willow.
       G          D7  G                 Am          B7
Write this on my tomb, that in love I was true.   Chorus
```

SECTION THREE

HAMMERING-ON

Technique

A note may be played by striking a string sharply with a finger of the *left* hand. This is called *hammering-on* and it is particularly useful and characteristic in certain types of song accompaniments.

Finger a C chord.

Keeping the first and third fingers down on their respective notes, lift the second finger off the D string. Play the open D string. Bring the second finger down sharply on the second fret. You should hear the note E quite clearly. Then follow with an up pluck with the fingers, as per normal, on the first three strings.

We can make a "complete" strum out of this by preceding this hammer-on with a bass-chord strum. The hammer-on is equivalent in time to two eighth notes (of an arpeggio, for example).

Try the same thing with G7. The second finger hammers the A string.

Billy Boy

C
Oh, where does she live,
Billy Boy, Billy Boy?
Oh, where does she live,
G7
Charming Billy?
She lives on the hill,
C
Forty miles from the mill.
(F) (C)
She's a young thing,
G7 C
And cannot leave her mother.

C
Did she bid you to come in,
Billy Boy, Billy Boy?
Did she bid you to come in,
G7
Charming Billy?
Yes she bade me to come in,
C
And to kiss her on the chin.
(F) (C)
She's a young thing,
G7 C
And cannot leave her mother.

C
And did she take your hat,

Billy Boy, Billy Boy?

And did she take your hat,

G7
Charming Billy?

Oh yes, she took my hat,

C
And she threw it at the cat.

(F) (C)
She's a young thing,

G7 C
And cannot leave her mother.

C
Did she set for you a chair,

Billy Boy, Billy Boy?

Did she set for you a chair,

G7
Charming Billy?

Yes, she set for me a chair,

But the bottom wasn't there.

(F) (C)
She's a young thing,

G7 C
And cannot leave her mother.

C
Can she bake a cherry pie,

Billy Boy, Billy Boy?

Can she bake a cherry pie,

G7
Charming Billy?

She can bake a cherry pie,

C
Quick's a cat can wink her eye.

(F) (C)
She's a young thing,

G7 C
And cannot leave her mother.

C
Can she make a feather bed,

Billy Boy, Billy Boy?

Can she make a feather bed,

G7
Charming Billy?

She can make a feather bed,

That will rise above your head.

(F) (C)
She's a young thing,

G7 C
And cannot leave her mother.

With F, the second finger hammers on the third string. The thumb of the right hand must play the third string. The up pluck, then, is with the second and third fingers on the second and first strings, respectively.

The hammer-on may be followed with an arpeggio. In this case, since the hammer is equivalent to the first two notes of the arpeggio, what remains for the arpeggio proper are the last two notes. These last two notes may be played either with the first and second or the second and third fingers. Timing is very important here. The "one-two" of the bass-chord sets the pace for the "one-

and-two-and" of the hammer-on plus arpeggio. The first half of this strum is equal in time to the second half.

C
F
G7
T chord T H 1 2 T C T H 2 3 T C T H 1 2
Count: 1 2 3 & 4 & 1 2 3 & 4 & 1 2 3 & 4 &

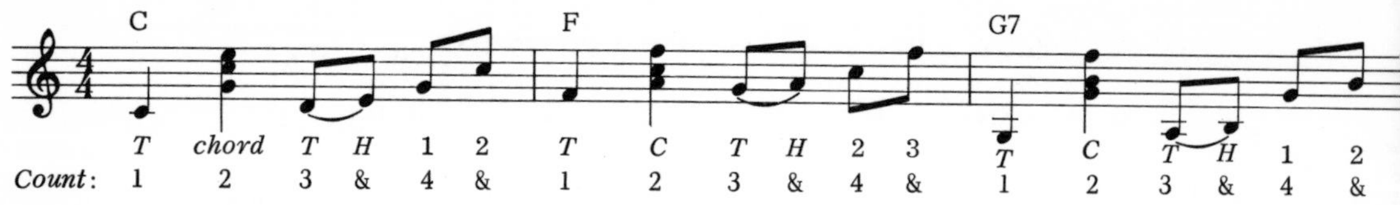

Father's Whiskers

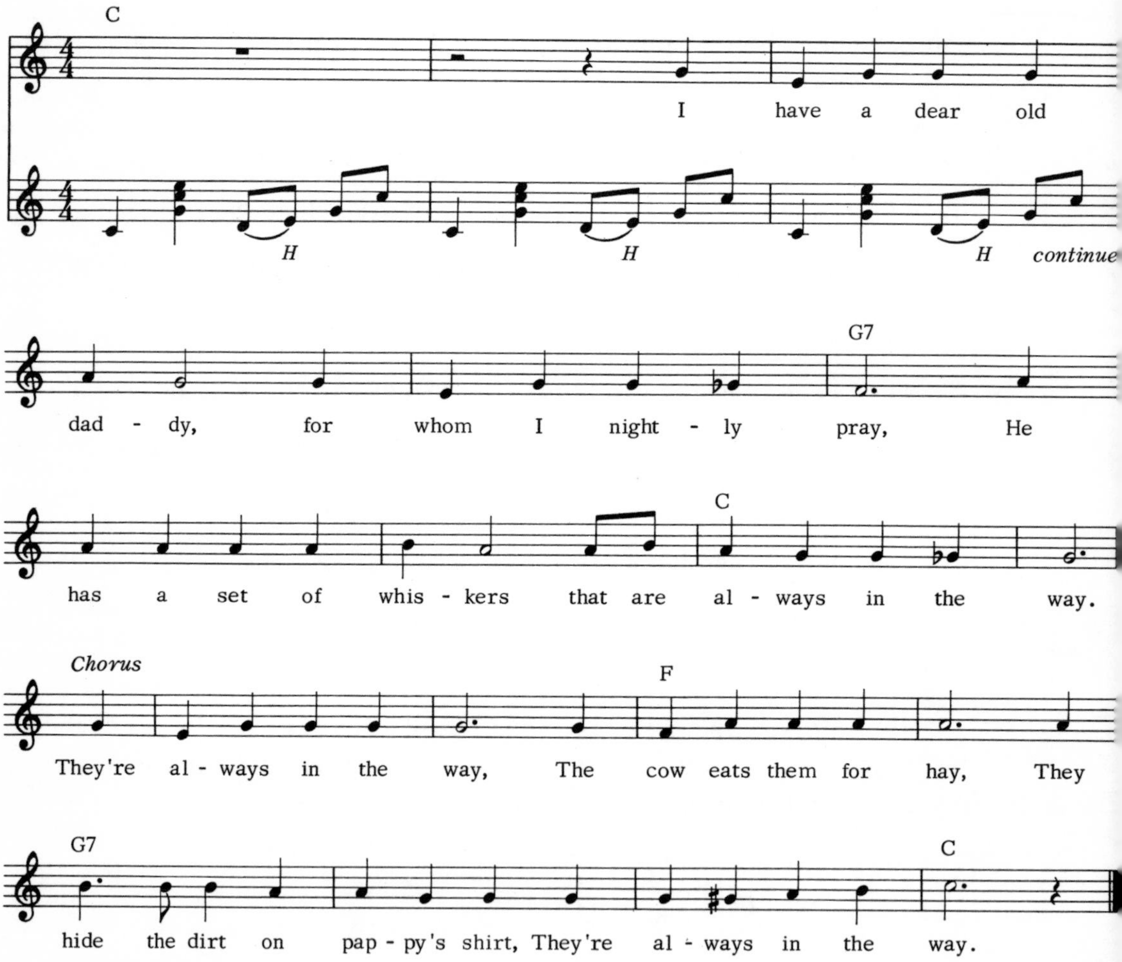

C
I have a dear old
H
H
H continue
dad - dy, for whom I night - ly
G7
pray, He
has a set of whis - kers that are
C
al - ways in the way.
Chorus
They're al - ways in the way, The
F
cow eats them for hay, They
G7
hide the dirt on pap - py's shirt, They're al - ways in the
C
way.

C
I have a dear old mother,
G7
With him at night she sleeps.
She wakes up in the morning,
C
Eating shredded wheat. *Chorus*

C
I have a dear old brother,
G7
He has a Ford machine.
He uses father's whiskers
C
To strain the gasoline. *Chorus*

C
Around the supper table,
G7
We make a happy group,
Until dear father's whiskers
C
Get tangled in the soup. *Chorus*

C
When Father goes in swimming,
G7
No bathing suit for him.
He ties his whiskers 'round his waist,
C
And gaily plunges in. *Chorus*

C
Father fought in Flanders,
G7
He wasn't killed, you see.
He hid behind his whiskers,
C
And fooled the enemy. *Chorus*

C
Father went out sailing,
G7
The wind blew down the mast.
He hoisted up his whiskers,
C
And never went so fast. *Chorus*

C
Father in a tavern,
G7
He likes his lager beer.
He pins a pretzel on his nose
C
To keep his whiskers clear. *Chorus*

Froggie Went A-Courting

Guitar rhythm:
H
H
H
C
Frog-gie went a-court-ing and he did ride, A-
hum, a-hum. Frog-gie went a-court-ing and he did ride, A
F
G7
C
sword and pis-tol by his side, A-hum, a-hum.

```
    C
He rode up to Miss Mousie's door,

      A-hum, a-hum.

He rode up to Miss Mousie's door,
         F             G7
Where he had often been before.
         C
      A-hum, a-hum.


    C
He said, "Miss Mouse, are you within?"

      A-hum, a-hum.

He said, "Miss Mouse, are you within?"
       F               G7
"Just lift the latch and please come in."
         C
      A-hum, a-hum.


    C
He took Miss Mousie on his knee,

      A-hum, a-hum.

He took Miss Mousie on his knee,
     F                           G7
And said, "Miss Mouse, will you marry me?"
         C
      A-hum, a-hum.


        C
"Without my uncle Rat's consent,"

      A-hum, a-hum.

"Without my uncle Rat's consent,
      F                G7
"I would not marry the president."
         C
      A-hum, a-hum.


        C
Now, uncle Rat, when he came home,

      A-hum, a-hum.

Now, uncle Rat, when he came home,
         F                   G7
Said, "Who's been here since I've been gone?"
         C
      A-hum, a-hum.
```

C
"A very fine gentleman has been here,"

A-hum, a-hum.

"A very fine gentleman has been here,
F G7
"Who wishes me to be his dear."
C
A-hum, a-hum.

C
Then uncle Rat laughed and shook his sides,

A-hum, a-hum.

Then uncle Rat laughed and shook his sides,
F G7
To think his niece would be a bride.
C
A-hum, a-hum.

C
So, uncle Rat, he went to town,

A-hum, a-hum.

Uncle Rat, he went to town
F G7
To buy his niece a wedding gown.
C
A-hum, a-hum.

C
Where will the wedding breakfast be?

A-hum, a-hum.

Where will the wedding breakfast be?
F G7
Away down yonder in the hollow tree.
C
A-hum, a-hum.

C
What will the wedding breakfast be?

A-hum, a-hum.

What will the wedding breakfast be?
F G7
Two green beans and a black-eyed pea.
C
A-hum, a-hum.

```
C
The first to come was the bumblebee,
     A-hum, a-hum.
The first to come was the bumblebee,
   F              G7
He danced a jig with Miss Mousie.
      C
     A-hum, a-hum.

  C
The next to come was Mister Drake,
     A-hum, a-hum.
The next to come was Mister Drake,
  F              G7
He ate up all of the wedding cake.
      C
     A-hum, a-hum.

   C
They all went sailing on the lake,
     A-hum, a-hum.
They all went sailing on the lake,
        F                       G7
And they all got swallowed by a big black snake.
      C
     A-hum, a-hum.

  C
So, that's the end of one, two, three,
     A-hum, a-hum.
That's the end of one, two, three—
    F                G7
The Rat, the Frog and Miss Mousie.
      C
     A-hum, a-hum.

       C
There's bread and cheese upon the shelf,
     A-hum, a-hum.
There's bread and cheese upon the shelf,
      F                    G7
If you want any more just sing it yourself.
      C
     A-hum, a-hum.
```

For G, the same note is hammered on as for G7.

G
Way up on the hill there's an old whisky still
C G
That is run by a hard-working crew.

You can tell if you sniff and you get a good whiff
D7 G
That they're making that old mountain dew. *Chorus*

```
    G
The preacher came by with a tear in his eye.
  C                            G
He said that his wife had the flu.

We told him he ought to give her a quart
        D7                   G
Of that good old mountain dew.   Chorus
```

```
G
My brother Mort is sawed off and short,
  C                     G
He measures just four foot two;

But he thinks he's a giant when they give him a pint
        D7                   G
Of that good old mountain dew.   Chorus
```

```
G
My uncle Bill has a still on the hill,
            C                 G
Where he runs off a gallon or two.

The birds in the sky get so high they can't fly,
        D7                   G
On that good old mountain dew.   Chorus
```

```
G
My aunty June has a brand new perfume,
 C                          G
It has such a sweet-smelling pu.

Imagine her surprise when she had it analyzed—
       D7                    G
It was good old mountain dew.   Chorus
```

```
G
Mister Roosevelt told me just how he felt
    C                            G
The day that the dry law went through:

"If your likker's too red, it will swell up your head—
        D7                       G
"Better stick to that mountain dew."   Chorus
```

For E minor, either bass note may be hammered.

The Butcher Boy

Em

She went up - stairs ___

H H H continue

___ to ___ make her bed, ___ And not a word ___ to her moth - er

G

Em

said, ___ Her moth - er she ___ went ___ up - stairs too, ___

G Em

___ Say - ing, "Daugh - ter, oh, daugh - ter, ___ what ___ trou - bles you?"

Em
"Oh Mother, oh Mother, I cannot tell,
G Em
"That butcher boy I love so well.
"He courted me my life away,
G Em
"And now at home he will not stay."

Em
"There is a place in London Town,
G Em
"Where that butcher boy goes and sits down.
"He takes that strange girl on his knee,
G Em
"And tells her what he won't tell me."

Em
Her father he came up from work,
G Em
Saying, "Where is daughter, she seems so hurt?"

He went upstairs to give her hope,
G Em
And found her hanging from a rope.

Em
He took his knife and cut her down,
G Em
And in her bosom these words he found:

"Go dig my grave both wide and deep,
G Em
"Place a marble slab at my head and feet.
Em
"And over my coffin place a snow-white dove,
G Em
"To warn the world I died of love."

Am
Paul and Silas bound in jail,
E7 Am
Had nobody for to go their bail.

Keep your hand on the plow,

Hold on. *Chorus*

Am
Paul and Silas begin to shout,
E7 Am
Jail doors opened and they walked out.

Keep your hand on that plow,

Hold on. *Chorus*

For A minor, the D string is hammered. For E7, hammer the A string.

Hold On

Am

Mar - y wore three links of chain, Ev - 'ry

H H H *continue*

E7 Am

link was Je - sus' name. Keep your hand on - a that

Chorus E7 Am

plow, Hold on.____ Hold on,____ Hold on,____

____ Keep your hand on - a that plow, Hold on.

Am
Peter was so nice and neat,
E7 Am
Wouldn't let Jesus wash his feet,

Keep your hand on the plow,

Hold on. *Chorus*

Am
Peter got anxious and he said,
E7 Am
"Wash my feet, hands and head."

Keep your hand on the plow,

Hold on. *Chorus*

Am
Jesus said, "If I wash them not,
E7 Am
"You'll have no father in this lot."

Keep your hand on the plow,

Hold on. *Chorus*

Am
Got my hand on the gospel plow,
E7 Am
Wouldn't take nothin' for my journey now.

Keep your hand on the plow,

Hold on. *Chorus*

SECTION FOUR

THE BANJO BRUSH

Technique

There are a variety of strums involving down- and/or up-brushing movements over the strings. The so-called "*banjo brush*" is one of the most useful of these.

Finger an E chord.

Pluck the bass E string in the normal manner with the thumb. Brush downward over the first four or five strings with the nails.

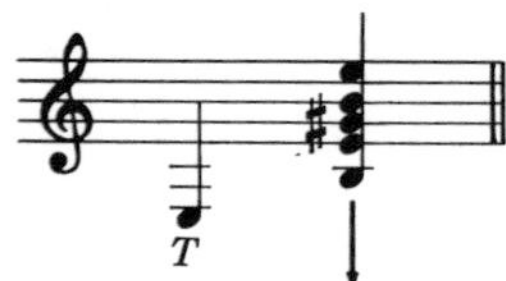

Repeat this—but now brush up with the index finger over the first few strings (the exact number doesn't matter). Timing is important here, as in any strum. The rhythm is *not* "one-two-three"—the three component parts of this strum are not equal. The down-up part may be thought of as two eighth notes if the bass note is a quarter note.

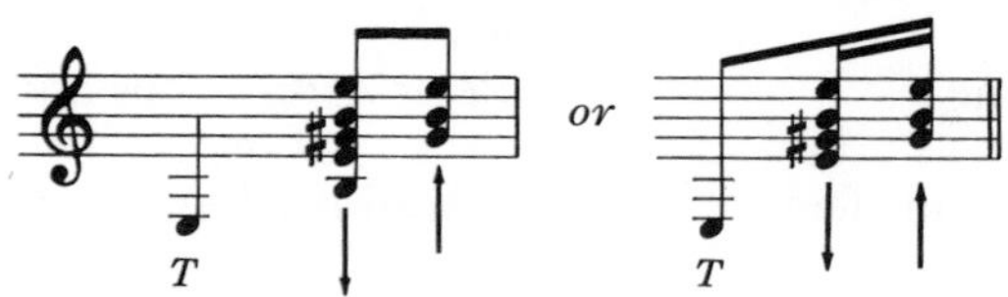

Columbus Stockade

E
'Way___ down___ in Co-lum-bus,
continue
B7 E
Geor-gia, Wan-na go back to Ten-nes-see.___
___ 'Way___ down___ in Co-lum-bus stock-
B7 E Chorus
ade, My friends all turned their backs on me.___ Well, you can
A E A
go and leave me if you want to, Nev-er
E B7 E
let me cross your mind,___ For in your heart___ you love an-
B7 E
oth-er, Leave, lit-tle dar-ling, I don't mind.

E
Many hours with you I've rambled,
B7 E
Many nights with you I've spent alone.
Now you've gone, you've gone and left me,
B7 E
And broken up our happy home. *Chorus*

E
Last night as I lay sleeping
B7 E
I dreamt I held you in my arms.
When I woke I was mistaken—
B7 E
I was peeping through the bars. *Chorus*

Lonesome Valley

Guitar rhythm:
A
Alternate basses throughout.
You've got to walk ___ that lone-some val-ley, ___ You've got to walk ___ it by your-self. ___ Ain't no-bo-dy here ___ can walk it for you, ___ You've got to walk that lone-some val-ley ___ by your-self.
E7
A A7
D
A
B7
E7
A

A
Your mother's got to walk that lonesome valley,
E7 A
She's got to walk it by herself.
A7 D A
Ain't nobody else can walk it for her—
B7 E7 A
She's got to walk that lonesome valley by herself.

A
Your father's got to walk that lonesome valley,
E7 A
He's got to walk it by himself.
A7 D A
Ain't nobody else can walk it for him—
B7 E7 A
He's got to walk that lonesome valley by himself.

A
Your brother's got to walk that lonesome valley,
E7 A
He's got to walk it by himself.
A7 D A
Ain't nobody else can walk it for him—
B7 E7 A
He's got to walk that lonesome valley by himself.

A
If you cannot preach like Peter,
E7 A
If you cannot pray like Paul,
A7 D A
You can tell the love of Jesus,
B7 E7 A
You can say He died for all.

The banjo brush may be used in conjunction with hammering-on.

Play a G chord.

Hammer on the fifth string—and follow with the down-up of the brush. All four component parts should be equal in time value.

A complete strum would have a banjo brush without the hammer-on followed by the banjo brush with the hammer-on.

Down by the Riverside

G

I'm gon - na lay down my

H H H

sword and shield, Down by the riv - er - side,— D7 Down by the

riv - er - side,— G Down by the riv - er - side,— Gon - na lay down my

sword and shield, Down by the riv - er - side,— And D7 stu - dy

Chorus
G
C
war no more. I ain't gon - na stu - dy war no
G
1. D7
more, I ain't gon-na stu-dy war no more, I ain't gon-na stu-dy___
G
2. D7
G
war no more I ain't gon-na stu - dy war no more.

```
        G
I'm gonna put on my long white robe,
Down by the riverside,
D7
Down by the riverside,
G
Down by the riverside.
I'm gonna put on my long white robe,
Down by the riverside,
     D7               G
And study war no more.    Chorus
```

```
          G
I'm gonna talk with the Prince of Peace,
Down by the riverside,
D7
Down by the riverside,
G
Down by the riverside.
I'm gonna talk with the Prince of Peace,
Down by the riverside,
     D7               G
And study war no more.    Chorus
```

```
          G
I'm gonna join hands with everyone,
Down by the riverside,
D7
Down by the riverside,
G
Down by the riverside.
I'm gonna join hands with everyone,
Down by the riverside,
     D7               G
And study war no more.    Chorus
```

Use hammer-on with the brush in the following song.

There Is a Tavern in the Town

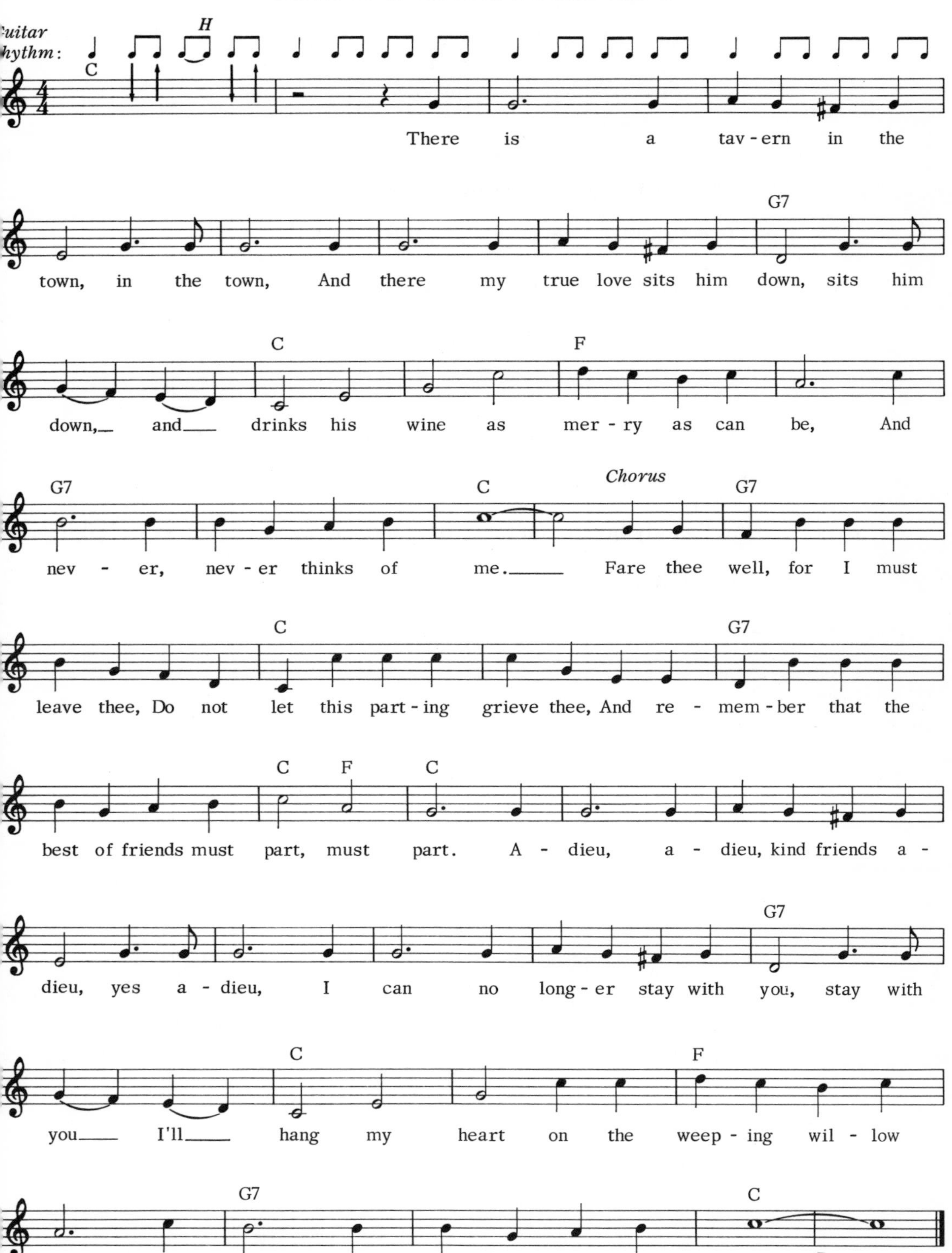

Guitar rhythm:
H
C
There is a tav - ern in the
town, in the town, And there my true love sits him down, sits him
G7
down, and drinks his wine as mer - ry as can be, And
C
F
G7
nev - er, nev - er thinks of me.
C
Chorus
G7
Fare thee well, for I must
leave thee, Do not let this part - ing grieve thee, And re - mem - ber that the
C
G7
best of friends must part, must part. A - dieu, a - dieu, kind friends a -
C
F
C
dieu, yes a - dieu, I can no long - er stay with you, stay with
G7
you I'll hang my heart on the weep - ing wil - low
C
F
tree, And may the world go well with thee.
G7
C

C
He left me for a damsel dark, damsel dark.
G7
Each Friday night they used to spark, used to spark.
C F
And now my love who once was true to me,
G7 C
Takes this dark damsel on his knee. *Chorus*

C
And now I see him nevermore, nevermore.
G7
He never knocks upon my door, on my door.
C F
Oh, woe is me, he pinned a little note,
G7 C
And these were all the words he wrote: *Chorus*

C
Oh, dig my grave both wide and deep, wide and deep.
G7
Put tombstones at my head and feet, head and feet.
C F
And on my breast you may carve a turtle dove,
G7 C
To signify I died for love. *Chorus*

SECTION FIVE

BASS RUNS

Another aspect of the variety that can be introduced into folk guitar accompaniments is the *bass run.* The bass run is a series of notes, played on the lower strings, coming at the point where one chord changes to another. Generally, the notes which make up the run are the notes of the scale which connect the roots of the two chords involved. The root of a chord is that note which gives the chord its letter name.

In $\frac{2}{4}$ or $\frac{4}{4}$ time the run begins two beats before the new chord is to be played. The run takes the place of the last two beats of the preceding chord and produces a smooth transition between the chords.

At this point the ability to read music would be of great help, so those of you who cannot already do so would be well advised to spend some time with Section Eight acquainting yourselves with the fundamentals of note reading.

To make things easier, though, I will give the string and fret numbers in this section for the notes of the runs. The first number is the string and the second number is the fret. For example: 4/0 = fourth string, open; 4/2 = fourth string, second fret.

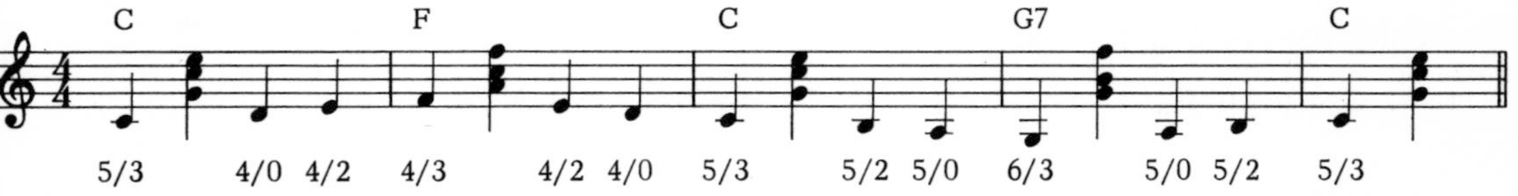

Frankie and Johnny

C
Frankie and Johnny went walking,

Johnny in his brand-new suit.
F
"Oh, good Lord," said Frankie,
C
"Don't my Johnny man look cute?"
G7 C
He was her man, but he done her wrong.

C
Johnny said, "I've got to leave you,

"But I won't be very long.
F
"Don't wait up for me, honey,
C
"Or worry while I'm gone."
G7 C
He was her man, but he done her wrong.

C
Frankie went down to the corner

To get a bucket of beer.
F
She said to the fat bartender,
C
"Has my lovin' man been here?"
G7 C
He was her man, but he done her wrong.

C
"Well, I ain't gonna tell you a story,

"I ain't gonna tell you no lie.
F
"I saw your Johnny 'bout an hour ago
C
"With a gal named Nellie Bly."
G7 C
He was her man, but he done her wrong.

C
Oh, Frankie got off at South Twelfth Street,
Looked up in a window so high,
F
And there she saw her Johnny
C
A-huggin' that Nellie Bly.
G7 C
He was her man, but he done her wrong.

C
Frankie pulled out her six-shooter,
Pulled out her old forty-four.
F
Her gun went rooty-toot-toot-toot,
C
And Johnny rolled over the floor.
G7 C
He was her man, but he done her wrong.

C
"Oh, roll me over so easy,
"Oh, roll me over so slow.
F
"Oh, roll me over easy, boys,
C
"For my wounds, they hurt me so—
G7 C
"I was her man, but I done her wrong."

C
Frankie got down on her knees,
Took Johnny into her lap.
F
She started to hug and kiss him,
C
But there was no bringing him back.
G7 C
He was her man, but he done her wrong.

C
"Oh, get me a thousand policemen,
"Oh, throw me into your cell,
F
" 'Cause I've shot my Johnny so dead,
C
"I know I'm going to hell."
G7 C
He was her man, but he done her wrong.

C
Roll out your rubber-tired carriage,
Roll out your old-time hack.
F
There's twelve men goin' to the graveyard,
C
And eleven coming back.
G7 C
He was her man, but he done her wrong.

Union Train

```
    C
It's that union train a-coming, coming, coming,
    G7              C
It's that union train a-coming, coming, coming,
    F               C
It's that union train a-coming, coming, coming,
            G7      C
   Get on board, get on board.
```

C
It has saved a-many a thousand, thousand, thousand,
G7 C
It has saved a-many a thousand, thousand, thousand,
F C
It has saved a-many a thousand, thousand, thousand,
G7 C
Get on board, get on board.

C
It will carry us to freedom, freedom, freedom,
G7 C
It will carry us to freedom, freedom, freedom,
F C
It will carry us to freedom, freedom, freedom,
G7 C
Get on board, get on board.

C
It will carry us to vict'ry, vict'ry, vict'ry,
G7 C
It will carry us to vict'ry, vict'ry, vict'ry,
F C
It will carry us to vict'ry, vict'ry, vict'ry,
G7 C
Get on board, get on board.

C
Let us join the one big union, union, union,
G7 C
Let us join the one big union, union, union,
F C
Let us join the one big union, union, union,
G7 C
Get on board, get on board.

Runs in $\frac{3}{4}$ time

In $\frac{3}{4}$ and $\frac{6}{8}$ the run usually begins three beats before the new chord is to be played. The run takes the place of the last three beats of the preceding chord.

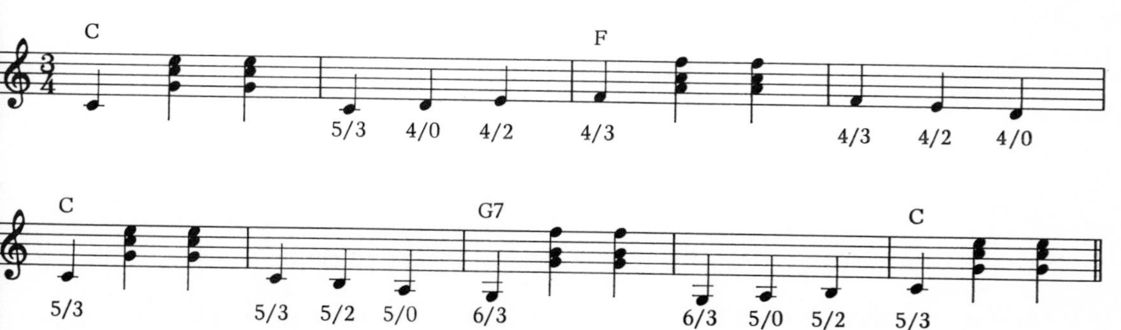

The Cruel Youth

C F
There was a youth, a cruel youth; He lived be-
Guitar:
5/3 4/0 4/2 4/3

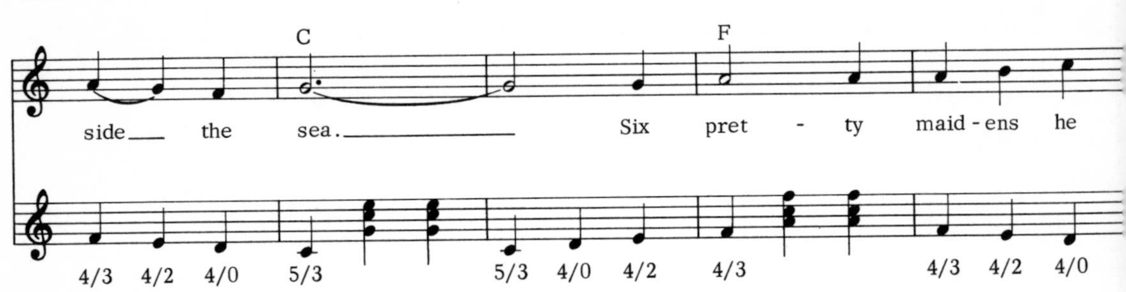
C F
side the sea. Six pretty maidens he
4/3 4/2 4/0 5/3 5/3 4/0 4/2 4/3 4/3 4/2 4/0

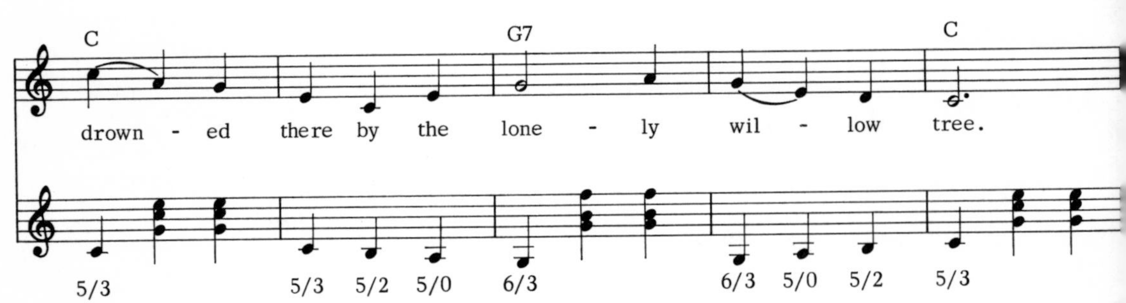
C G7 C
drowned there by the lonely willow tree.
5/3 5/3 5/2 5/0 6/3 6/3 5/0 5/2 5/3

C
As he walked forth with Sally Brown,
F C
As he walked the sea,
F C
An evil thought then came to him
G7 C
By that lonely willow tree.

C
"But first take off your golden gown,
F C
"Take off your gown," said he;
F C
"For though I am going to murder you,
G7 C
"I would not spoil your finery."

C
"Now, turn your back to the waterside,
F C
"Your face to the willow tree;
F C
"Six pretty maidens I drowned here,
G7 C
"And you the seventh shall be.

C
"Then turn around, you false young man,
F C
"Then turn around," said she;
F C
"For it is not meet that such a youth
G7 C
"A naked woman should see."

C
'hen ’round he turned, that false young man,
C
Round about turned he,
F C
nd seizing him boldly in both her arms,
G7 C
he cast him into the sea.

C
“Lie there, lie there, you false young man,
F C
“Lie there, lie there,” said she;
F C
“For six pretty maidens you’ve drowned here,
G7 C
“Go keep them company.”

C
He sank beneath the icy waves,
F C
He sank down into the sea;
F C
No living thing wept a tear for him
G7 C
Save that lonely willow tree.

The Strawberry Roan

C
G7
I was hang - in' 'round town just a - spend - ing my time. Noth - ing else
Guitar:
5/3 5/2 5/0 6/3
C
to spend not ev - en a dime, When a fel - ler steps up and he
6/3 5/0 5/2 5/3
5/3 4/0 4/2
F
G7
says "I sup - pose you're a bronc - bust - in' man___ by the looks of your
4/3
6/3 5/0 5/2

C
G7
clothes." "You guessed me right, and a good one," I claim, "Do you
5/3 5/3 5/2 5/0 6/3
C
hap - pen to have an - y bad ones to tame?" He says, "I've got
6/3 5/0 5/2 5/3
F
G7
one and a bad one to buck; At throw - in' bronc rid - ers, he's
5/3 4/0 4/2 4/3
Chorus
C
G7
C
had lots of luck, Well, it's Oh, that straw - ber - ry roan!
6/3 5/0 5/2 5/3 5/3 5/2 5/0 6/3 5/3 4/0 4/2
F
C
F
Oh, that straw - ber - ry roan! He says, "This old
4/3 4/3 4/2 4/0 5/3 5/3 4/0 4/2 4/3

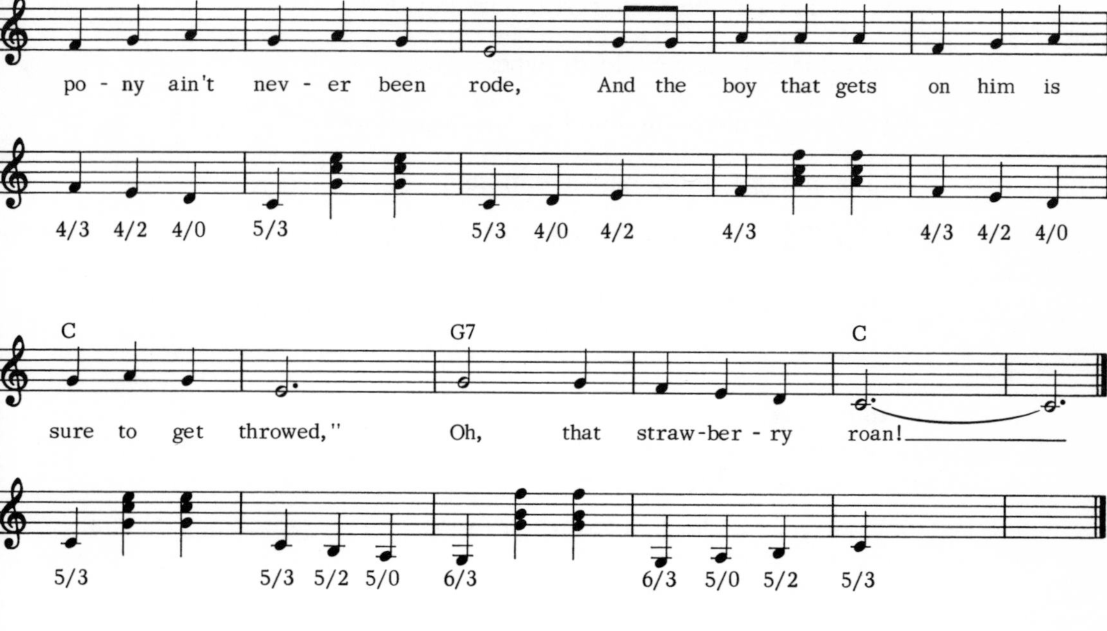
C F
po - ny ain't nev - er been rode, And the boy that gets on him is
4/3 4/2 4/0 5/3 5/3 4/0 4/2 4/3 4/3 4/2 4/0
C G7 C
sure to get throwed," Oh, that straw-ber - ry roan!
5/3 5/3 5/2 5/0 6/3 6/3 5/0 5/2 5/3

C G7
I gets all excited and asks what he pays
C
To ride this old goat for a couple of days.
F
He offers a ten spot. I says, "I'm your man,
G7 C
"For the bronc never lived that I couldn't fan;
G7
"No, the bronc never lived, nor he never drew breath
C
"That I couldn't ride till he starved plumb to death."
F
He says, "Get your saddle, I'll give you a chance."
G7 C
We got in the buckboard and drove to the ranch.

Chorus:

G7 C
Well, it's Oh, that strawberry roan,
F C
Oh, that strawberry roan!
F C
We stayed until morning, and right after chuck
F C
We goes out to see how this outlaw can buck,
G7 C
Oh, that strawberry roan.

C G7
Well, down in the horse corral standing alone
C
Was that old cavayo, old strawberry roan.
F
His legs were spavined and he had pigeon toes,
G7 C
Little pig eyes and a big Roman nose.
G7
Little pin ears that were crimped at the tip,
C
With a big "forty-four" branded 'cross his left hip.
F
He's ewe-necked and old, with a long lower jaw,
G7 C
You can see with one eye he's a reg'lar outlaw.

Chorus:
G7 C
Well, it's Oh, that strawberry roan,
F C
Oh, that strawberry roan!
F C
He's ewe-necked and old, with a long lower jaw,
F C
You can see with one eye he's a reg'lar outlaw,
G7 C
Oh, that strawberry roan.

C G7
Well, I put on my spurs and I coils up my twine,
C
I piled my loop on him—I'm sure feeling fine.
F
I piled my loop on him and well I knew then,
G7 C
If I rode this old pony, I'd sure earn my ten.
G7
I put the blinds on him—it sure was a fight,
C
Next comes the saddle, I screws her down tight.
F
I gets in his middle and opens the blind,
G7 C
I'm right in his middle to see him unwind.

Chorus:
G7 C
Well, it's Oh, that strawberry roan,
F C
Oh, that strawberry roan!
F C
He lowered his neck and I think he unwound,
F C
He seemed to quit living there down on the ground,
G7 C
Oh, that strawberry roan.

```
        C                            G7
He went up towards the east and came down towards the west,
                          C
To stay in his middle I'm doin' my best.
                                F
He's about the worst bucker I've seen on the range—
       G7                                C
He can turn on a nickel and give you some change,
                             G7
He turns his old belly right up to the sun,
                           C
He sure is one sun-fishin' son of a gun!
                                F
I'll tell you, no foolin', this pony can step,
        G7                                 C
But I'm still in his middle and buildin' a rep.

    Chorus:
                        G7         C
    Well, it's Oh, that strawberry roan,
    F                   C
    Oh, that strawberry roan!
            F                         C
    He goes up on all fours and comes down on his side,
      F                            C
    I don't see what keeps him from losing his hide.
    G7                  C
    Oh, that strawberry roan!

  C                    G7
I loses my stirrup and also my hat,
                             C
I starts pulling leather, I'm blind as a bat.
                          F
With a big forward jump he goes up on high,
          G7                                C
Leaves me sittin' on nothin' way up in the sky.
                             G7
I turns over twice and comes back to the earth,
                          C
I lights in a-cussin' the day of his birth.
                             F
I know there are ponies I'm unable to ride—
G7                                      C
Some are still living, they haven't all died.

    Chorus:
                        G7         C
    Well, it's Oh, that strawberry roan,
    F                   C
    Oh, that strawberry roan!
         F                    C
    I'll bet all my money the man ain't alive
             F                        C
    That can stay with old strawberry making his dive,
    G7                  C
    Oh, that strawberry roan!
```

Runs in G

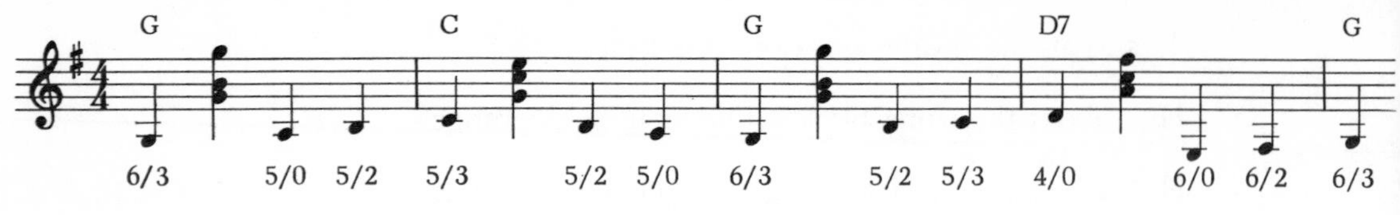

Seeing Nellie Home

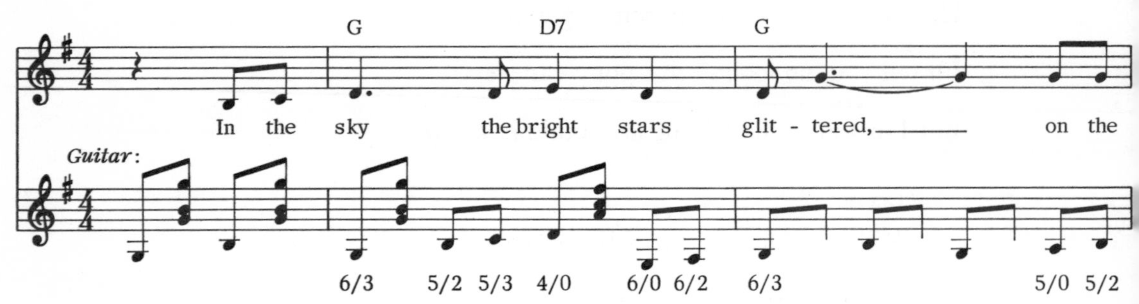

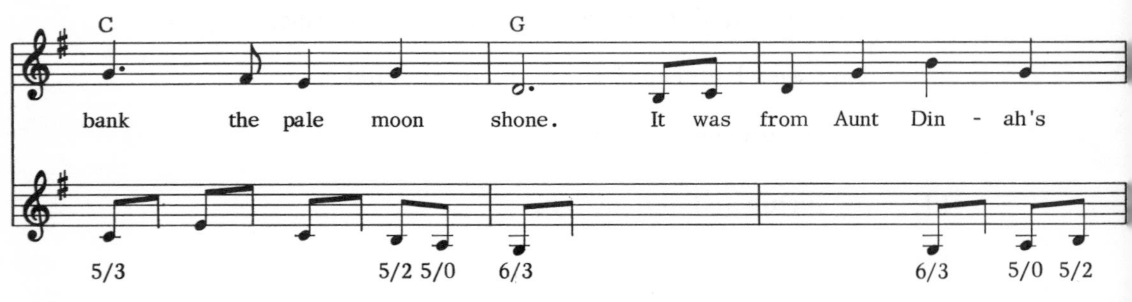

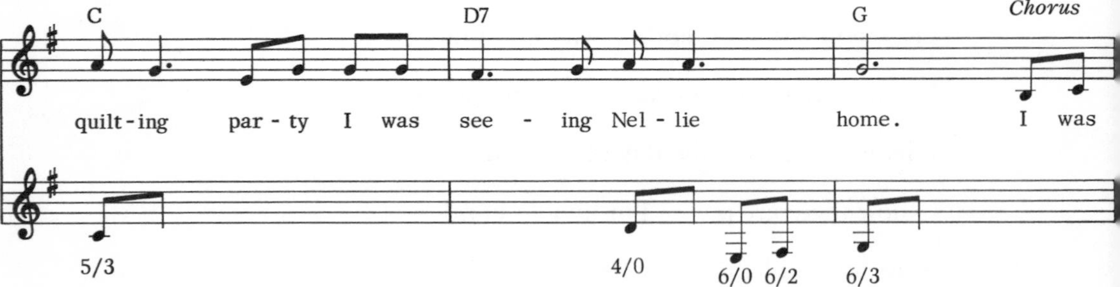

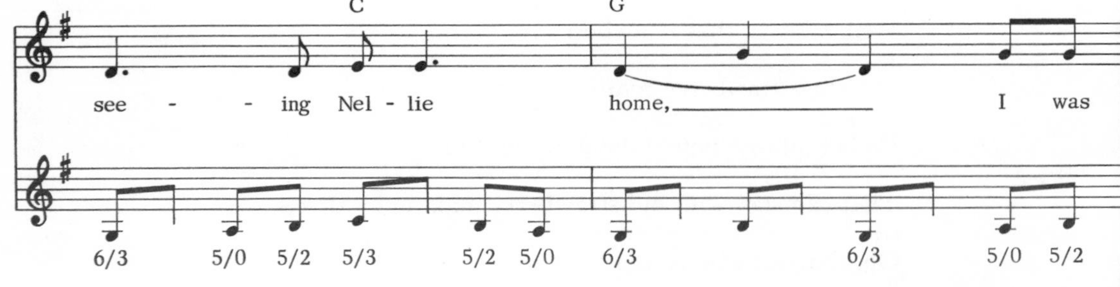

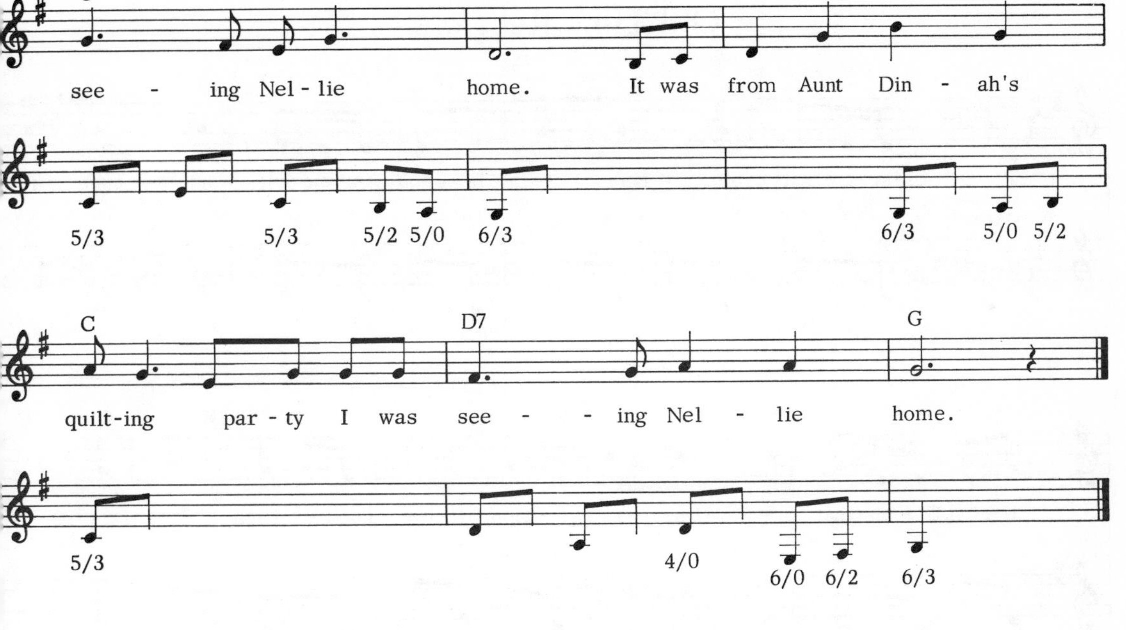

G D7 G
On my arm a soft hand rested,
C G
Rested light as ocean foam.
C
It was from Aunt Dinah's quilting party,
D7 G
I was seeing Nellie home. *Chorus*

G D7 G
On my lips a whisper trembled,
C G
Trembled till it dared to come.
C
It was from Aunt Dinah's quilting party,
D7 G
I was seeing Nellie home. *Chorus*

G D7 G
On my life new hopes were dawning,
C G
And those hopes have lived and grown.
C
It was from Aunt Dinah's quilting party,
D7 G
I was seeing Nellie home. *Chorus*

Old Time Religion

G
D7
Gim-me that old time re - li gion, Gim-me that old time re -
Guitar:
6/3 5/2 5/3 4/0
G
C
D7
G
li-gion, Gim-me that old time re - li - gion, It's good e-nough for me.
4/0 6/0 6/2 6/3 5/0 5/2 5/3 5/3 5/4 4/0

G
It was good for the Hebrew children,
D7
It was good for the Hebrew children,
G C
It was good for the Hebrew children,
D7 G
It's good enough for me.

G
It was good for Paul and Silas,
D7
It was good for Paul and Silas,
G C
It was good for Paul and Silas,
D7 G
It's good enough for me.

G
It'll be good when the world's on fire,
D7
It'll be good when the world's on fire,
G C
It'll be good when the world's on fire,
D7 G
It's good enough for me.

Runs in $\frac{3}{4}$ time.

G C
6/3 5/0 5/2 5/3 5/3 5/2 5/0
G D7 G
6/3 6/3 5/2 5/3 4/0 4/0 6/0 6/2 6/3

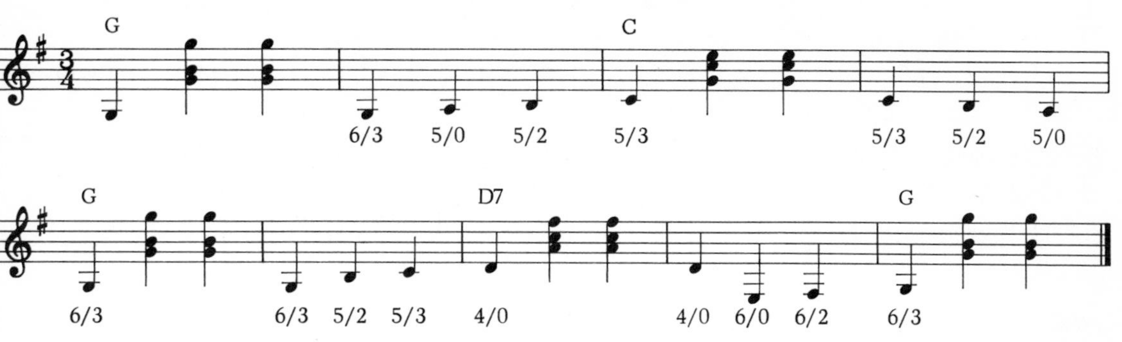

Engine 143

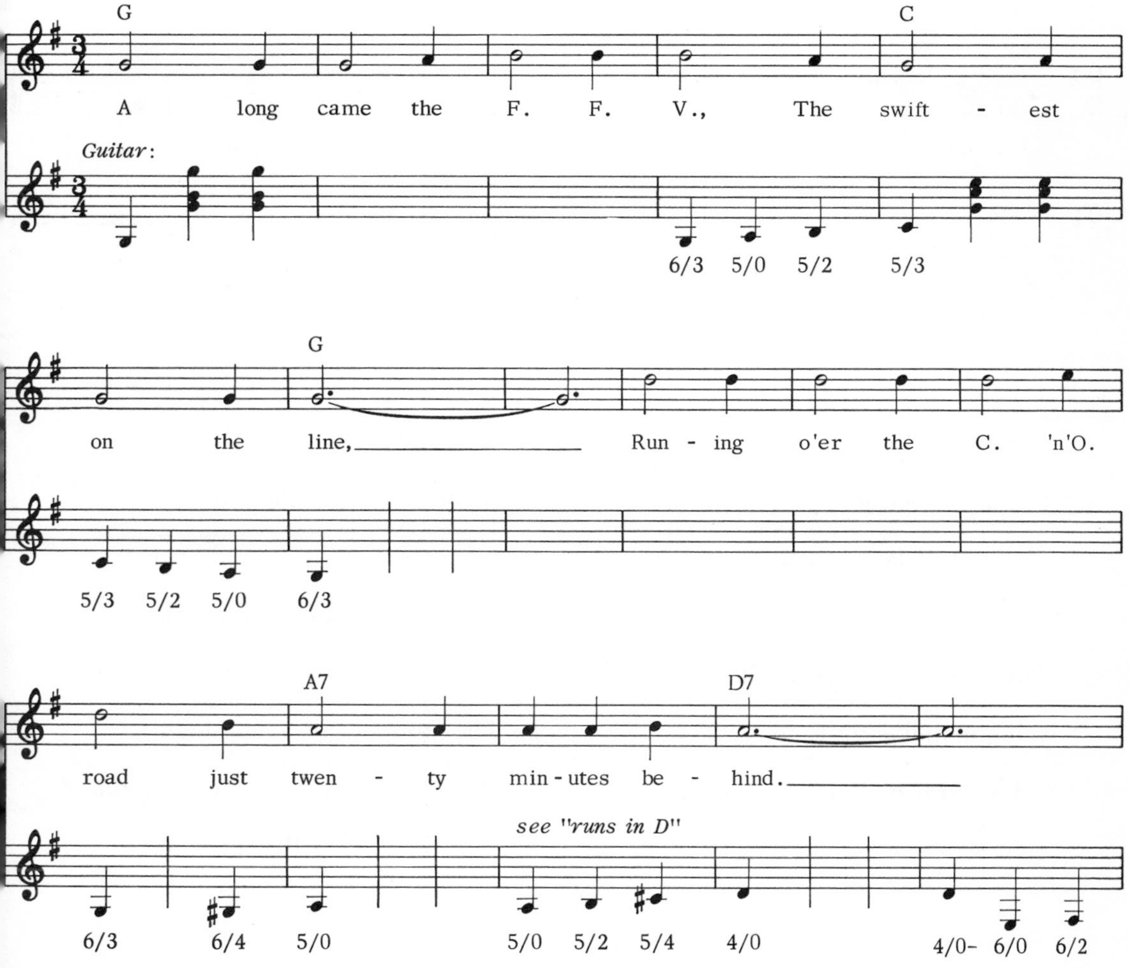

G C
A long came the F. F. V., The swift - est
Guitar:
6/3 5/0 5/2 5/3
G
on the line, Run - ing o'er the C. 'n'O.
5/3 5/2 5/0 6/3
A7 D7
road just twen - ty min - utes be - hind.
see "runs in D"
6/3 6/4 5/0 5/0 5/2 5/4 4/0 4/0- 6/0 6/2

G
Georgie's mother came to him,
C G
A bucket on her arm.

Saying to her darling son,
A7 D7
"Be careful how you run.
G
"Many a man has lost his life
C G
"Trying to make lost time,
C G
"And if you run your engine right,
D7 G
"You'll get there just on time."

G
Up the road she darted,
C G
Against the rock she crushed.

Upside down the engine turned
A7 D7
And Georgie's head did smash.
G
His head against the fire-box door,
C G
The flames were rolling high.
C G
"I'm glad I was born for an engineer,
D7 G
"On the C & O Road to die."

G
The doctor said to Georgie,
C G
"My darling boy, be still,

"Your life it may yet be saved
A7 D7
"If it is God's blessed will."
G
"Oh, no," said George, "that will not do,
C G
"I want to die so free,
C G
"I want to die for the engine I love—
D7 G
"One Hundred and Forty-Three."

G
The doctor said to Georgie,
C G
"Your life cannot be saved.

"Murdered upon a railroad,
A7 D7
"And laid in a lonesome grave."
G
His face was covered up with blood,
C G
His eyes they could not see,
C G
And the very last words poor George said
D7 G
Were, "Nearer, my God, to Thee."

Poor Boy

G D7 G G7
As I walked down to the riv-er, poor boy, to
Guitar:
6/3 5/2 5/3 4/0 6/0 6/2 6/3 6/3 5/0 5/2
C G
see the ships go by, My sweet-heart stood on the
5/3 5/3 5/2 5/0 6/3
D7 G
Chorus
deck of one, and she waved to me good - bye. Bow
6/3 5/2 5/3 4/0 4/0 6/0 6/2 6/3

D7 G G7 C
down your head and cry, poor boy, Bow down your
6/3 5/2 5/3 4/0 6/0 6/2 6/3 6/3 5/0 5/2 5/3

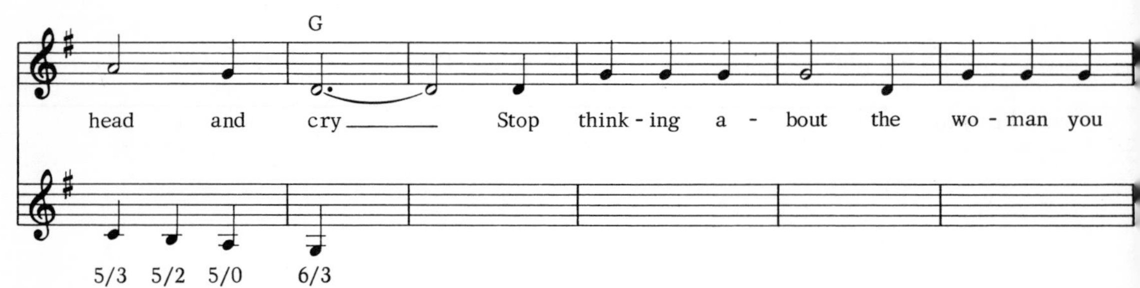
G
head and cry___ Stop think-ing a-bout the wo-man you
5/3 5/2 5/0 6/3

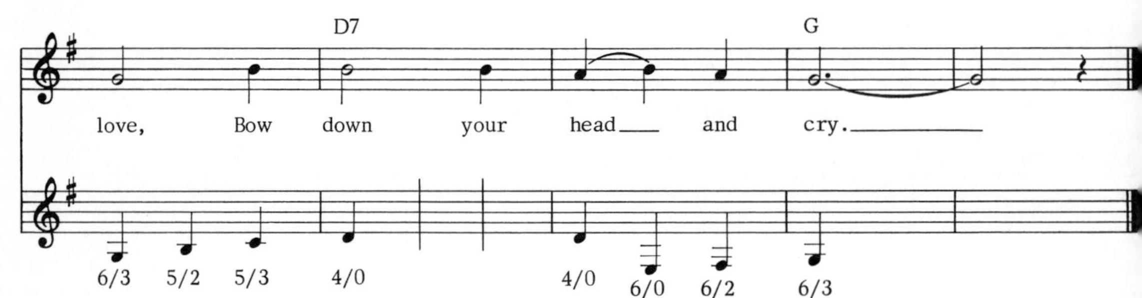
D7 G
love, Bow down your head___ and cry.___
6/3 5/2 5/3 4/0 4/0 6/0 6/2 6/3

G D7 G G7
I follered her for months and months,
C G
She offered me her hand.
We were just about to get married,
D7 G
When she ran off with a gambling man. *Chorus*

G D7 G G7
He come at me with a big jack knife;
C G
I went at him with lead.
When the fight was over, poor boy,
D7 G
He lay down beside me dead. *Chorus*

G D7 G G7
They took me to the big jail house;
C G
The months and months rolled by.
The jury found me guilty, poor boy,
D7 G
And the judge said, "You must die." *Cho*

G D7 G G7
And yet they call this justice, poor boy,
C G
Then justice let it be.
I only killed a man that was
D7 G
Just a-fixing to kill me. *Chorus*

Runs in D

Jennie Jenkins

D A7 D

Will you wear red, oh my dear, oh my dear, Oh, will you wear red, Jen-nie

Guitar:

4/0 5/4 5/2 5/0 5/2 5/4 4/0 5/4 5/2

A7 D G *Chorus*

Jen-kins? No, I won't wear red, it's the col-or of my head, I'll

5/0 5/2 5/4 4/0 6/0 6/2 6/3 5/2 5/4

D G D

buy me a fol-di-rol-di, til-di-tol-di, seek a dou-ble use a co-zy roll to

4/0 6/0 6/2 6/3 5/2 5/4 4/0

A7 D

find me, Roll, Jen-nie Jen-kins roll.

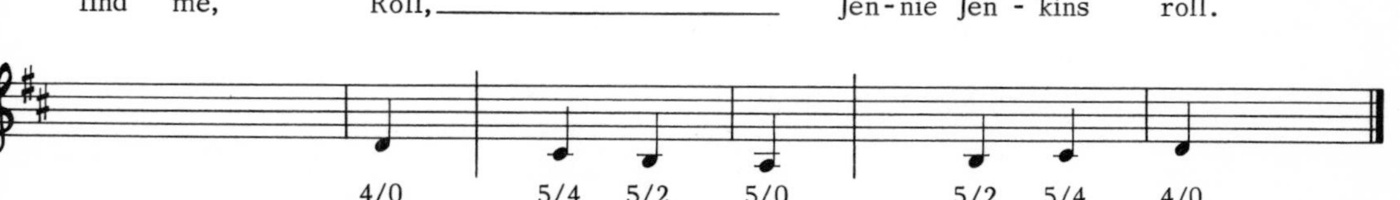

D   A7
Oh, will you wear white, oh my dear, oh my dear?
D   A7
Oh, will you wear white, Jennie Jenkins?
          D
    No, I won't wear white,
               G
    For the color's too bright.   *Chorus*

D   A7
Will you wear green, oh my dear, oh my dear?
D   A7
Will you wear green, Jennie Jenkins?
          D
    No, I won't wear green—
         G
    It's a shame to be seen.   *Chorus*

D   A7
Will you wear blue, oh my dear, oh my dear?
D   A7
Will you wear blue, Jennie Jenkins?
          D
    No, I won't wear blue,
               G
    For the color's too true.   *Chorus*

D   A7
Will you wear yellow, oh my dear, oh my dear?
D   A7
Will you wear yellow, Jennie Jenkins?
          D
    No, I won't wear yellow,
             G
    For I'd never get a fellow.   *Chorus*

D   A7
Will you wear brown, oh my dear, oh my dear?
D   A7
Will you wear brown, Jennie Jenkins?
          D
    No, I won't wear brown,
             G
    For I'd never get around.   *Chorus*

D   A7
Will you wear beige, oh my dear, oh my dear?
D   A7
Will you wear beige, Jennie Jenkins?
          D
    No, I won't wear beige,
            G
    For it shows my age.   *Chorus*

D A7
Will you wear orange, oh my dear, oh my dear?
D A7
Will you wear orange, Jennie Jenkins?

D
No, orange I won't wear,
G
And it rhymes—so there! *Chorus*

D A7
What will you wear, oh my dear, oh my dear?
D A7
What will you wear, Jennie Jenkins?

D
Oh, what do you care
G
If I just go bare? *Chorus*

The Mermaid

D G D
'Twas Fri - day morn when we set sail, And we
Guitar:
4/0 6/0 6/2 6/3 5/2 5/4 4/0 6/0 6/2
G A7 D
were not far from the land, When our cap - tain spied a
6/3 6/3 6/4 5/0 5/2 5/4 4/0 4/0 6/0 6/2
G D G A7 D Chorus
love - ly mer - maid with a comb and a glass in her hand. Oh, the
6/3 5/2 5/4 4/0 6/0 6/2 6/3 6/3 6/4 5/0 5/2 5/4 4/0

A7
o - cean waves may roll, And the storm - y seas may blow, while_
4/0 5/4 5/2 5/0 5/0 5/2 5/4
D G D G A7
we poor_ sail-ors go skip-ing to the top, And the land - lub-bers lie down be -
4/0 6/0 6/2 6/3 5/2 5/4 4/0 6/0 6/2 6/3 6/3 6/4 5/0 5/2 5/4
D G A7 D
low, be-low, be-low, And the land - lub-bers lie down be - low.
4/0 6/0 6/2 6/3 6/3 6/4 5/0 5/2 5/4 4/0

D G D
Then up spake the captain of our gallant ship,
G A7 D
And a well-spoken man was he.
G D
"I have me a wife in Salem town,
G A7 D
"And tonight she a widow will be." *Chorus*

D G D
Then up spake the cook of our gallant ship,
G A7 D
And a well-spoken cook was he.
G D
"I care much more for my kettles and my pots
G A7 D
"Than I do for the bottom of the sea." *Chorus*

D G D
Then up spake the cabin boy of our gallant ship,
G A7 D
And a well-spoken youth was he.
G D
"There's nary a soul in Salem town
G A7 D
"Who cares a bit for me." *Chorus*

D G D
Then three times around went our gallant ship,
G A7 D
And three times around went she.
G D
Then three times around went our gallant ship,
G A7 D
And she sank to the bottom of the sea. *Chorus*

Runs in $\frac{3}{4}$ time.

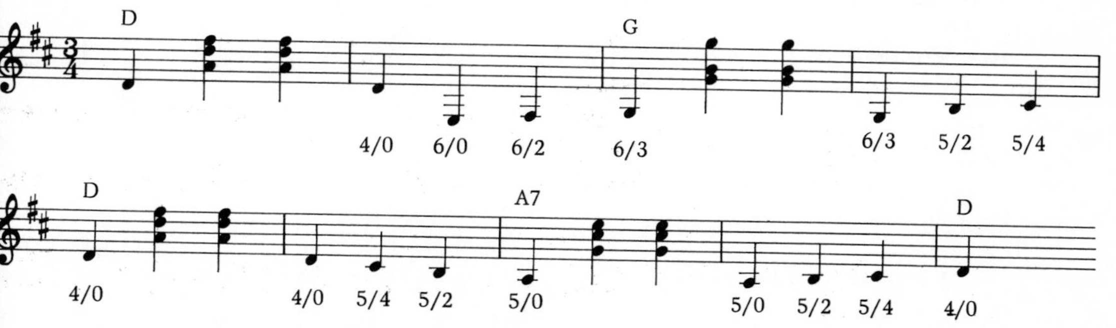

Cryderville Jail

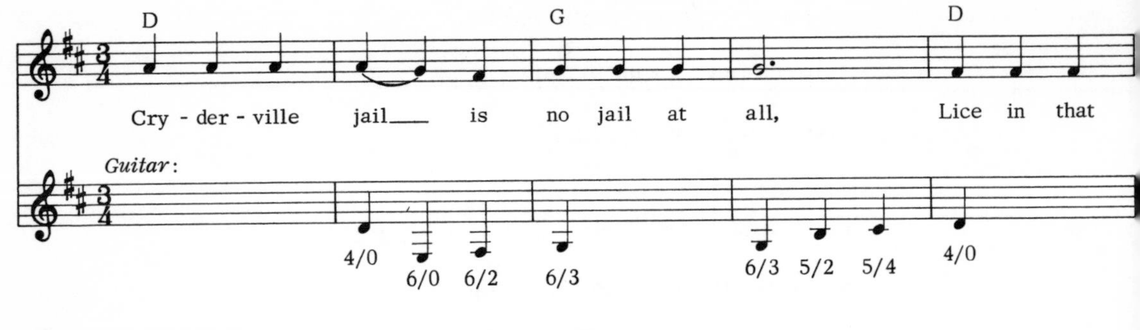

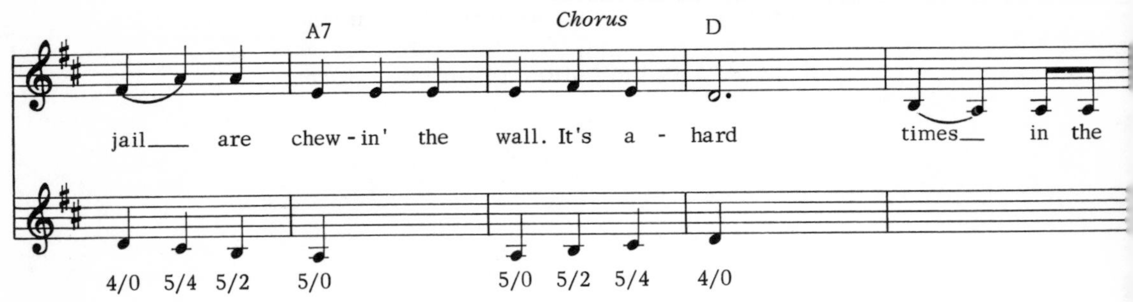

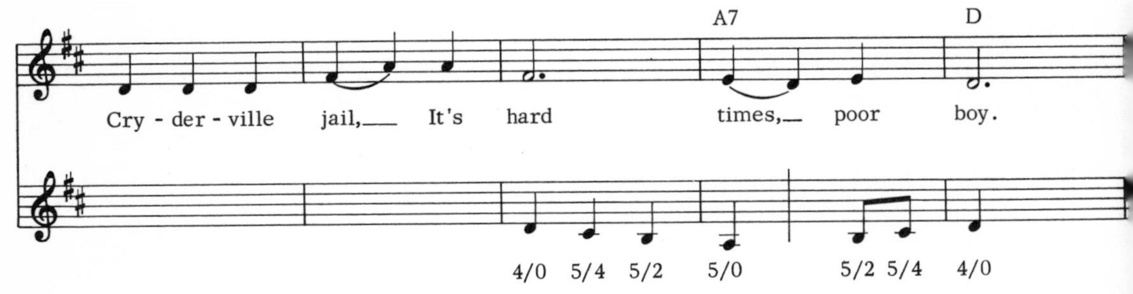

D
There's a big bull ring
G
In the middle of the floor,
D
And a damned old jailer
A7
To open the door. *Chorus*

D
Your pockets he'll pick,
G
Your clothes he will sell.
D
Your hands he will handcuff—
A7
Goddamn him to hell! *Chorus*

D
Our bed it is made
G
Of old rotten rugs.
D
And when we lie down
A7
We are covered with bugs. *Chorus*

D
The bugs, they swear,
G
If we don't make bail,
D
We are bound to get busy
A7
In Cryderville Jail. *Chorus*

D
I wrote to my mother
G
To send me a knife,
D
For the lice and the chinches
A7
Have threatened my life. *Chorus*

D
And here's to the lawyer,
G
He'll come to your cell,
D
And swear he will clear you
A7
In spite of all hell. *Chorus*

D
Get all your money
G
Before he will rest.
D
Then say, "Plead guilty,
A7
"For I think it the best." *Chorus*

D
Old Judge Simpkins
G
Will read us the law.
D
The damndest fool judge
A7
That you ever saw. *Chorus*

D
And there sits the jury,
G
A devil of a crew.
D
They'll look a poor prisoner
A7
Clean through and through. *Chorus*

D
And here's to the sheriff,
G
I like to forgot,
D
The damndest old rascal
A7
We have in the lot. *Chorus*

D
Your privileges he'll take,
G
Your clothes he will sell.
D
Get drunk on the money—
A7
Goddamn him to hell! *Chorus*

D
And now I have come
G
To the end of my song.
D
I'll leave it to the boys
A7
As I go along. *Chorus*

I've Got No Use for Women

D
My pal was a straight young cowpuncher,
G D
Honest and upright and square.
G D
But he turned to a gambler and gunman,
Em A7
And a woman sent him there.
D
He fell in with evil companions,
G D
The kind that are better off dead.
G D
When a gambler insulted her picture,
A7 D
He hauled off and filled him with lead.

D
All through the long night they trailed him
G D
Through mesquite and thick chaparral,
G D
And I couldn't help cursing that woman
Em A7
As I saw him pitch, stagger and fall.
D
If she'd been the pal that she should have,
G D
He might have been raising a son,
G D
Instead of out there on the prairie
A7 D
To die by the cruel ranger's gun.

D
all a - like at the bot - tom
G
Self - ish and
4/0
4/0 6/0 6/2 6/3
grasp - ing for
D
all.
They'll
G
stick by a
man when he's
6/3 5/2 5/4
4/0
4/0 6/0 6/2
6/3
6/3 5/2 5/4
D
win - ning,
And
A7
laugh in his
face when he
D
falls.
4/0
4/0 5/4 5/2
5/0
5/0 5/2 5/4
4/0

D
Death's slow sting did not trouble—
G D
His chances for life were too slim.
G D
But where they were putting his body
Em A7
Was all that worried him.
D
He lifted his head on his elbow,
G D
The blood from his wound flowed bright red.
G D
He looked at his pals grouped around him,
A7 D
And whispered to them and said:

D
"Oh, bury me out on the prairie,
G D
"Where the coyotes may howl o'er my grave,
G D
"Bury me out on the prairie,
Em A7
"And some of my bones please save.
D
"Wrap me up in my blanket
G D
"And cover me deep 'neath the ground,
G D
"Cover me over with boulders
A7 D
"Of granite, huge and round."

D
So they buried him out on the prairie,
G D
And the coyotes still howl o'er his grave,
G D
But his soul is now a-resting
Em A7
From the unkind cut she gave.
D
And many a similar cowpuncher,
G D
As he rides by that pile of stones,
G D
Recalls some similar woman,
A7 D
And envies his molding bones.

Runs in A

A D A E7 A
5/0 5/2 5/4 4/0 5/4 5/2 5/0 6/4 6/2 6/0 6/2 6/4 5/0

Lolly Too Dum

A
As I went out one morn ing to take the pleas - ant
Guitar:
5/0 6/4 6/2
E7 A E7
air, Lol - ly too dum, too dum, Lol - ly too dum
6/0 6/2 6/4 5/0 5/0 6/4 6/2 6/0 6/2 6/4

A
D
day, As I went out one morn - ing to take the pleas-ant
5/0 5/0 5/2 5/4 4/0
A
air, I ov - er-heard a moth - er, a - scold-ing her daugh-ter
4/0 5/4 5/2 5/0 5/0 6/4 6/2
E7 A E7 A
fair, Lol - ly too dum, too dum, Lol - ly too dum day.
6/0 6/2 6/4 5/0 5/0 6/4 6/2 6/0 6/2 6/4 5/0

A E7
"You better go wash them dishes, and hush that flattering tongue,"

A E7 A
Lolly too dum, too dum, lolly too dum day.

A D
"You better go wash them dishes, and hush that flattering tongue,

A E7
"You know you want to get married and that you are too young."

A E7 A
Lolly too dum, too dum, lolly too dum day.

A E7
"Oh, pity my condition just as you would your own,"

A E7 A
Lolly too dum, too dum, lolly too dum day.

D
"Oh, pity my condition just as you would your own,

A E7
"For fourteen long years I've been living all alone."

A E7 A
Lolly too dum, too dum, lolly too dum day.

A E7
"Supposin' I was willin', where would you get your man?"
A E7 A
Lolly too dum, too dum, lolly too dum day.
D
"Supposin' I was willin', where would you get your man?"
A E7
"Why, Lordy mercy, Mammy, I'd marry handsome Sam."
A E7 A
Lolly too dum, too dum, lolly too dum day.

A E7
"Supposin' he should slight you like you done him before?"
A E7 A
Lolly too dum, too dum, lolly too dum day.
D
"Supposin' he should slight you like you done him before?"
A E7
"Why, Lordy mercy, Mammy, I could marry forty more."
A E7 A
Lolly too dum, too dum, lolly too dum day.

A E7
"There's peddlers and tinkers and boys from the plow,"
A E7 A
Lolly too dum, too dum, lolly too dum day.
D
"There's peddlers and tinkers and boys from the plow,
A E7
"Oh, Lordy mercy, Mammy, I'm gettin' that feelin' now."
A E7 A
Lolly too dum, too dum, lolly too dum day.

A E7
"Now my daughter's married and well for to do."
A E7 A
Lolly too dum, too dum, lolly too dum day.
D
"Now my daughter's married and well for to do,
A E7
"Gather 'round young fellers, I'm on the market, too."
A E7 A
Lolly too dum, too dum, lolly too dum day.

Golden Slippers

A
Oh, my gold - en slip - pers are___ laid a - way, 'Cause I
long white robe___ that I bought last June I'm a -
Guitar:
don't 'spect to wear 'em till my wed - ding day, And my long tailed coat that I
goin' to get changed 'cause it fits too soon, And the old gray horse that I
E7
5/0 6/4 6/2 6/0
loved so well, I will wear up in the char-iot in the morn. And my
used to drive, I will hitch him to the char-iot in the
1.A
6/0 6/2 6/4 5/0
2. A
Chorus
D
morn. Oh, them gold - en slip-pers, Oh, them
5/0 5/0 5/2 5/4 4/0
E7
1.
A
gold - en slip-pers, Gold - en slip-pers I'm___ gon - na wear, Be - cause they look so
6/0 6/2 6/4 5/0

Oh, my old banjo hangs on the wall,
'Cause it ain't been tuned since 'way last fall,
But the folks all say we'll have a good time
When we ride up in the chariot in the morn.

There's old brother Ben and his sister Luce,
They will telegraph the news to Uncle 'Bacco Juice.
What a great camp meeting there will be that day,
When we ride up in the chariot in the morn. *Chorus*

So, it's good-by, children, I will have to go
Where the rain don't fall and the wind don't blow,
And your winter coats, why, you will not need,
When you ride up in the chariot in the morn.

But your golden slippers must be nice and clean,
And your age must be just sweet sixteen,
And your white kid gloves you will have to wear,
When you ride up in the chariot in the morn. *Chorus*

Runs in $\frac{3}{4}$ time.

A
D
5/0 5/2 5/4 4/0
4/0 5/4 5/2
A
E7
A
5/0
5/0 6/4 6/2 6/0
6/0 6/2 6/4 5/0

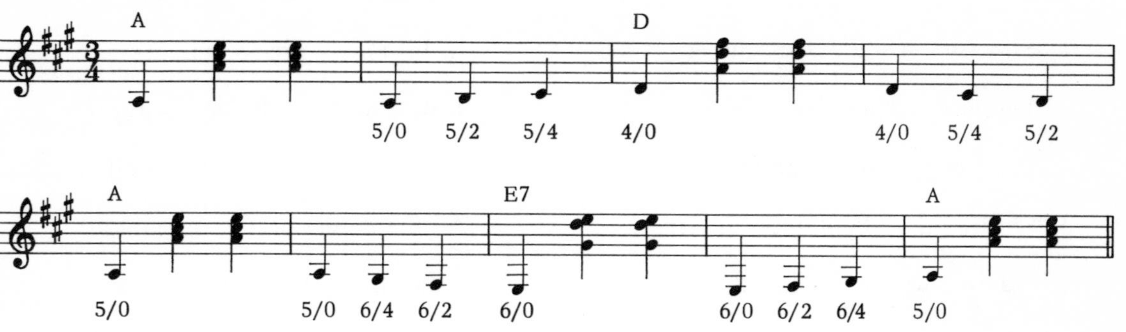

Kevin Barry

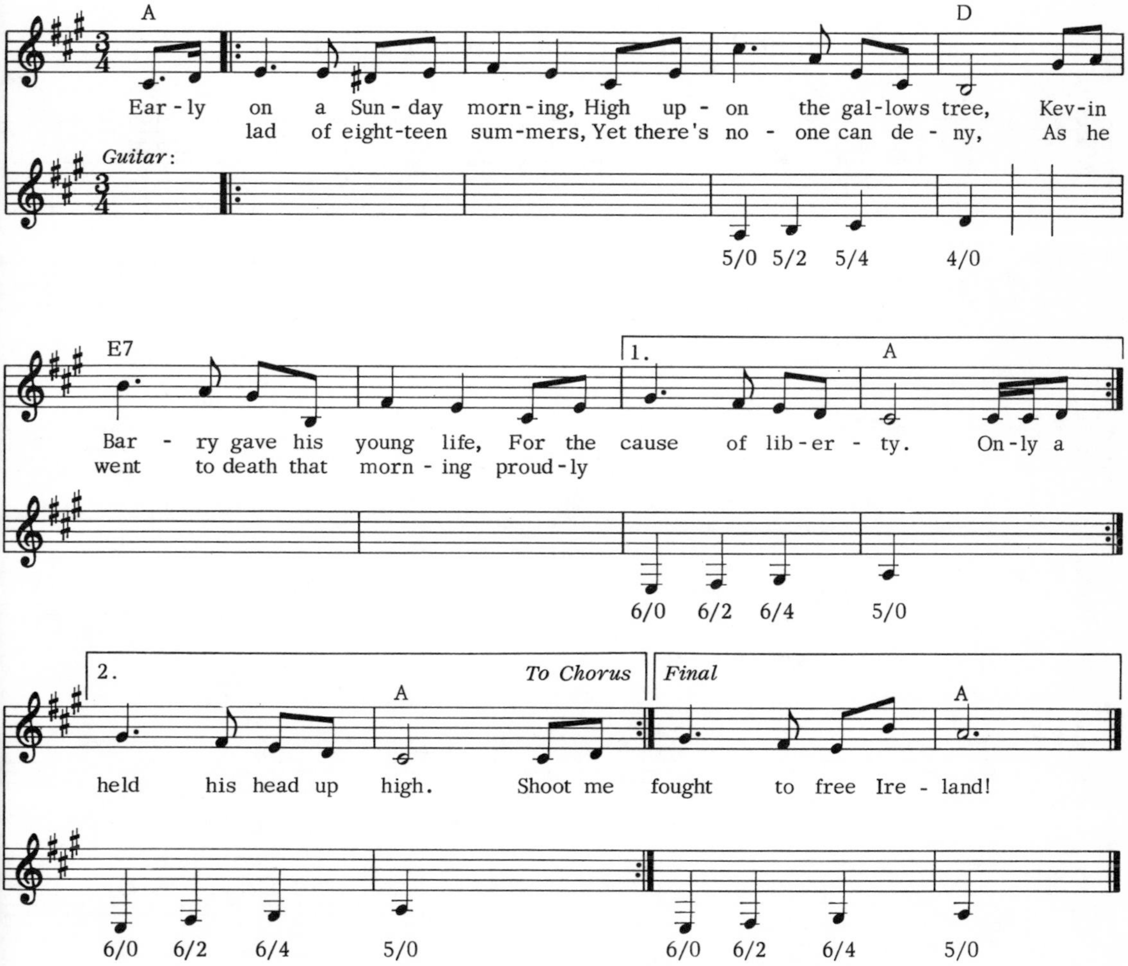

A
D
Ear-ly on a Sun-day morn-ing, High up-on the gal-lows tree, Kev-in
lad of eight-teen sum-mers, Yet there's no-one can de-ny, As he
Guitar:
5/0 5/2 5/4 4/0
E7
1.
A
Bar-ry gave his young life, For the cause of lib-er-ty. On-ly a
went to death that morn-ing proud-ly
6/0 6/2 6/4 5/0
2.
To Chorus
Final
A
A
held his head up high. Shoot me fought to free Ire-land!
6/0 6/2 6/4 5/0
6/0 6/2 6/4 5/0

Chorus:

"Shoot me like an Irish soldier,
"Do not hang me like a dog;
"For I fought for Ireland's freedom
"On that dark September morn—
"All around that little bakery,
"Where we fought them hand to hand.
"Shoot me like an Irish soldier,
"For I fought to free Ireland."

Just before he faced the hangman,
In his lonely prison cell,
British soldiers tortured Barry
Just because he would not tell
All the names of his companions—
Other things they wished to know.
"Turn informer and we'll free you."
Proudly, Barry answered, "No!"

Chorus

The Devil and the Farmer's Wife

A
D
The dev - il came up to the farm - er one day, Tee - roo, tee -
Guitar:
5/0 5/2 5/4 4/0
roo, to the farm - er one day, Says, "One of your fam' - ly I'm
4/0 5/4 5/2 5/0
E7
tak - ing a - way, Tee - roo, tee - roo, I'm tak - ing a - way.
5/0 6/4 6/2 6/0
6/0 6/2 6/4 5/0

        A
"Oh, please don't take my eldest son,
          D   A
    "Teeroo, teeroo, my eldest son,
                                                    E7
"There's work on the farm that's got to be done,
                                          A
    "Teeroo, teeroo, that's got to be done.

              A
"Take my wife, take my wife with the joy of my heart,
          D   A
    "Teeroo, teeroo, with the joy of my heart,
                                              E7
"And I hope, by golly, that you never part,
                                          A
    "Teeroo, teeroo, that you never part."

     A
The Devil put the old lady into a sack,
        D   A
    Teeroo, teeroo, into a sack,
                                         E7
And down the road he goes clickety-clack
                                          A
    Teeroo, teeroo, he goes clickety-clack.

              A
When the Devil got her to the fork in the road,
        D   A
    Teeroo, teeroo, to the fork in the road,
                                                 E7
He says, "Old woman, you're a hell of a load,
                                              A
    "Teeroo, teeroo, you're a hell of a load."

              A
When the Devil got her to the gates of hell,
        D   A
    Teeroo, teeroo, to the gates of hell,
                                                  E7
He says, "Poke up the fires, we'll bake her well,
                                         A
    "Teeroo, teeroo, we'll bake her well."

      A
Up came a little devil with a ball and chain,
        D   A
    Teeroo, teeroo, with a ball and chain,
                                                              E7
She upped with her foot and she kicked out his brains,
                                                A
    Teeroo, teeroo, she kicked out his brains.

A
Then nine little devils went climbing the wall,
D A
Teeroo, teeroo, went climbing the wall,
E7
Screaming, "Take her back, Daddy, she'll murder us all,
A
"Teeroo, teeroo, she'll murder us all."

A
The old man was peeping out of the crack,
D A
Teeroo, teeroo, peeping out of the crack.
E7
When he saw the old Devil come bringing her back,
A
Teeroo, teeroo, come bringing her back.

A
He says, "Here's your wife, both sound and well,
D A
"Teeroo, teeroo, both sound and well,
E7
"If I kept her there longer she'd have torn up hell,
A
"Teeroo, teeroo, she'd have torn up hell."

A
He says, "I've been a devil most all of my life,
D A
"Teeroo, teeroo, most all of my life,
E7
"But I've never been in hell till I met with your wife,
A
"Teeroo, teeroo, till I met with your wife."

A
This proves that the women are better than men,
D A
Teeroo, teeroo, are better than men.
E7
They can all go to hell and come back again,
A
Teeroo, teeroo, and come back again.

Runs in E

E
A
E
6/0 6/2 6/4 5/0 6/4 6/2 6/0 6/4 5/0
B7
E
B7
E
5/2 6/4 6/2 6/0 4/1 5/4 5/2 5/4 4/1 4/2

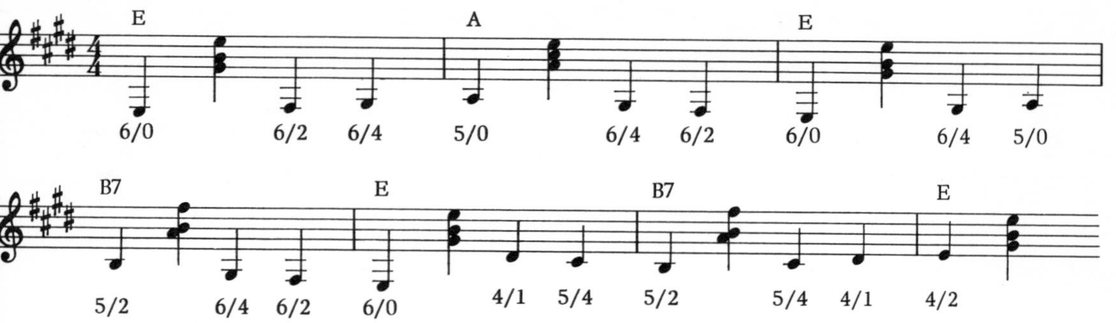

Little Old Sod Shanty on the Plain

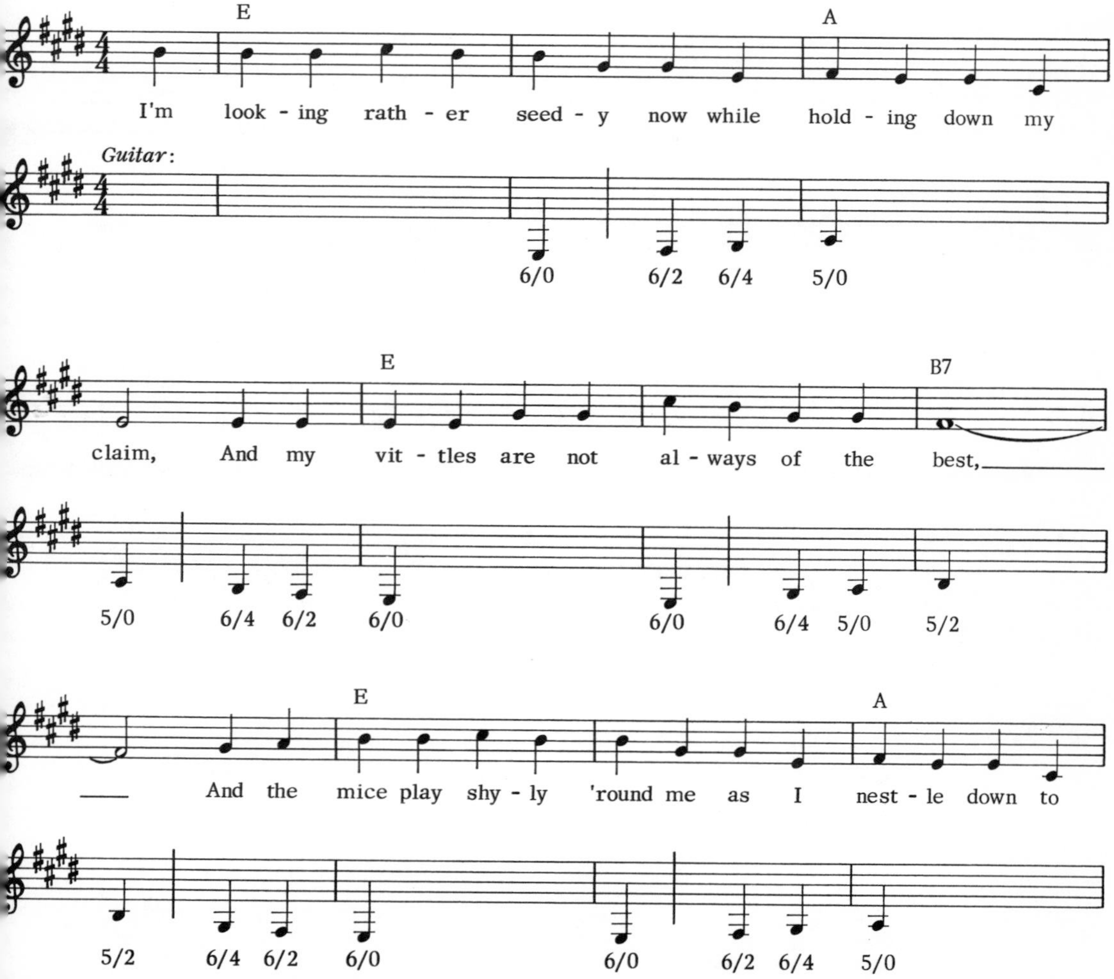

E
A
I'm look - ing rath - er seed - y now while hold - ing down my
Guitar:
6/0 6/2 6/4 5/0
E
B7
claim, And my vit - tles are not al - ways of the best,
5/0 6/4 6/2 6/0 6/0 6/4 5/0 5/2
E
A
And the mice play shy - ly 'round me as I nest - le down to
5/2 6/4 6/2 6/0 6/0 6/2 6/4 5/0

E B7 E
rest in my lit - tle old sod shan - ty on the plain
5/0 6/4 6/2 6/0 6/4 5/0 5/2 5/4 4/1 4/2 5/2
Chorus
A E
Oh, the hin - ges are of leath - er and the win - dows have no
6/0 6/2 6/4 5/0 5/0 6/4 6/2 6/0
B7
glass, The boards, they let the howl - ing bliz - zard in,
6/0 4/1 5/4 5/2
E A
You can see the hun - gry coy - ote as he sneaks up through the
5/2 6/4 6/2 6/0 6/0 6/2 6/4 5/0
E B7 E
grass to my lit - tle old sod shan - ty on the plain.
5/0 6/4 6/2 6/0 6/4 5/0 5/2 5/4 4/1 4/2

E A
I rather like the novelty of living in this way,
E B7
Though my bill of fare isn't always of the best,
E A
But I'm happy as a clam on the land of Uncle Sam,
E B7 E
In my little old sod shanty in the West. *Chorus*

Unfortunate Miss Bailey

E
B7
A cap - tain bold from Hal - i - fax, who dwelt in coun - try
Guitar:
6/0 6/4 5/0 5/2
E
B7
quar-ters, se - duced a maid, who hanged her - self one morn-ing in her
5/2 5/4 4/1 4/2 4/2 4/1 5/4 5/2
E
gar - ters, His wick - ed con-science smit - ed him, he lost his stom-ach
5/2 5/4 4/1 4/2 6/0 6/4 5/0

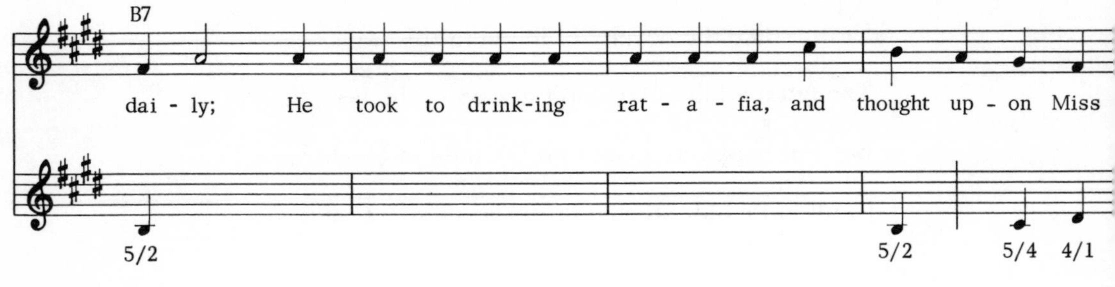

One night, betimes, he went to bed, for he had caught a fever,
Said he, "I am a handsome lad and I'm a gay deceiver."
His candle just at twelve o'clock began to burn quite palely,
A ghost stepped up to his bedside and said, "Behold! Miss Bailey!" *Chorus*

"Avaunt, Miss Bailey," then he cried, "You can't affright me really."
"Dear Captain Smith," the ghost replied, "you've used me ungenteelly.
"The coroner's 'quest was hard with me because I've acted frailly,
"And Parson Biggs won't bury me, though I'm a dead Miss Bailey." *Chorus*

"Miss Bailey, then, since you and I accounts must once for all close,
"I've got a five-pound note in my regimental small-clothes.
" 'Twill bribe the sexton for your grave." The ghost then vanished gaily,
Crying, "Bless you, wicked Captain Smith. Remember poor Miss Bailey." *Chorus*

Runs in $\frac{3}{4}$ time.

E
A
6/0 6/0 6/2 6/4 5/0 5/0 6/4 6/2
E
B7
6/0 6/0 6/4 5/0 5/2 5/2 6/4 6/2
E
B7
E
6/0 4/2 4/1 5/4 5/2 5/2 5/4 4/1 4/2

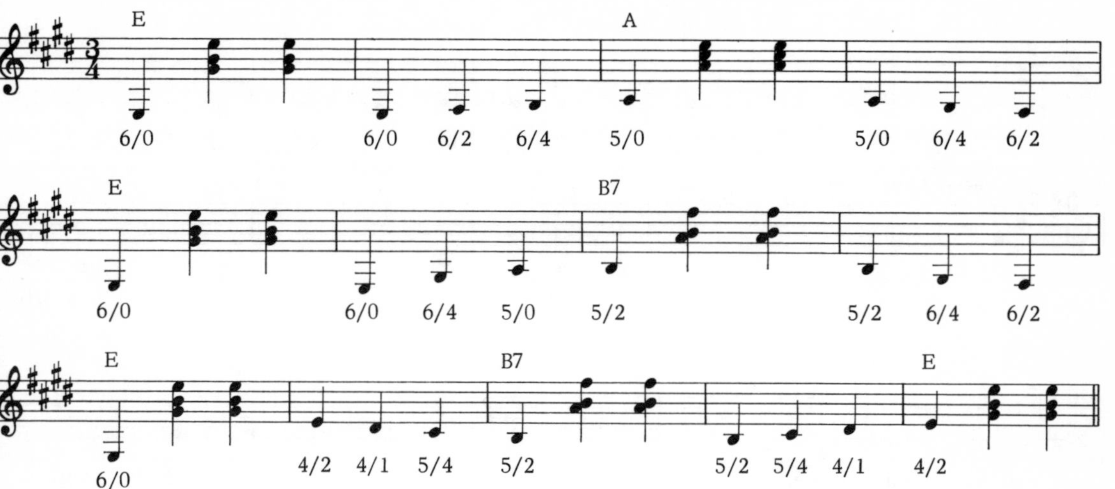

Oh, Brandy, Leave Me Alone

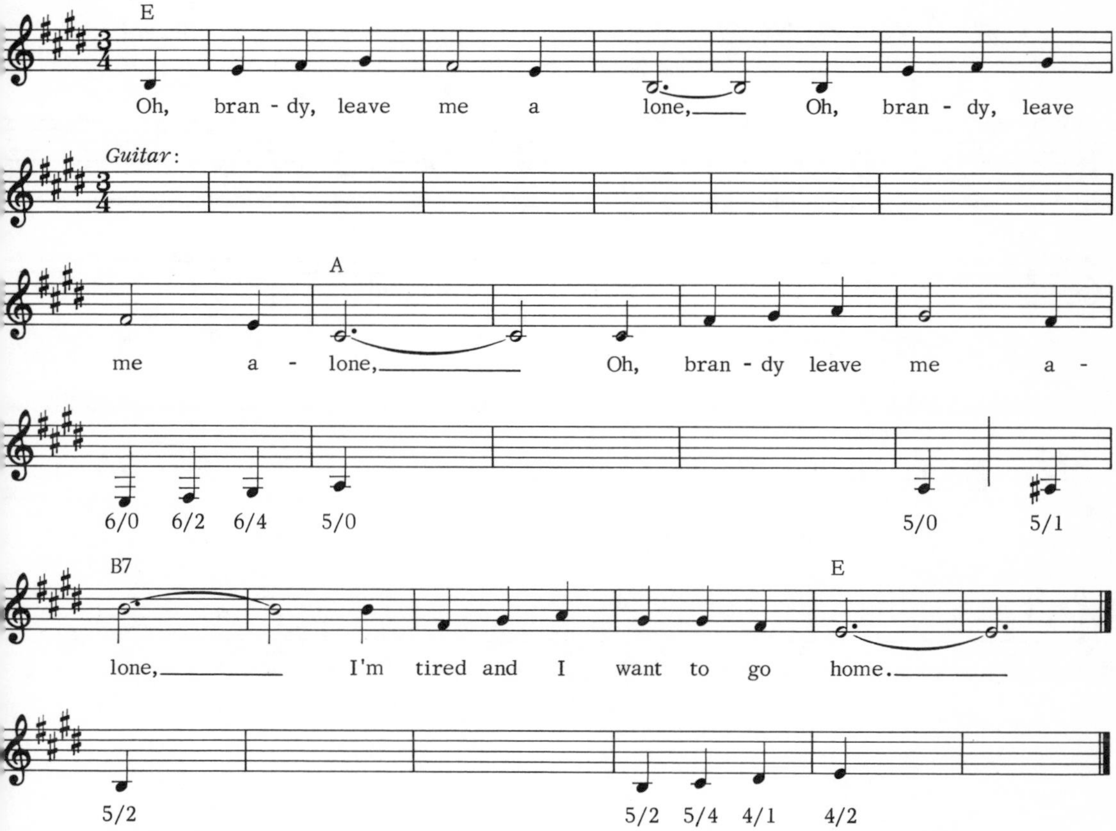

E
Oh, bran - dy, leave me a lone,
Oh, bran - dy, leave
Guitar:
A
me a - lone,
Oh, bran - dy leave me a -
6/0 6/2 6/4 5/0 5/0 5/1
B7
E
lone,
I'm tired and I want to go home.
5/2 5/2 5/4 4/1 4/2

Oh, brandy, you broke my heart. (E)
Oh, brandy, you broke my heart. (A)
Oh, brandy, leave me alone— (B7)
Remember I must go home. (E)

Likes Likker Better Than Me

B7 E
bring him back to me. Oh, bring me
4/2 4/1 5/4 5/2 5/2 5/4 4/1 4/2
A E B7 E
back my brown - eyed boy, Likes lik - ker bet - ter than me.
6/0 6/2 6/4 5/0 5/2 6/4 6/2 6/0

E A E
Last night he came to see me again,
B7 E
Last night he smiled on me,
A E
But tonight he smiles on a whisky jug—
B7 E
Likes likker better than me. *Chorus*

E A E
Sometimes I think I'll marry him,
B7 E
For I love him dearer than life.
A E
But, oh, it's all so hard to bear
B7 E
As a whisky drinker's wife. *Chorus*

SECTION SIX

BLUES

The blues is the great American song form. It combines elements of melodic contour, harmonic progression, rhythmic drive, instrumental technique, subject matter, and performance style into a rich blend, offering the student and the professional alike an endless source of inspiration and pleasure.

The instrumental technique—specifically, the guitar—is what most of all concerns us here. Blues guitar playing draws upon all the elements of folk guitar so far gone into in this volume and adds to them a healthy helping of its own personality. Our first consideration will be the rhythm—as exemplified by what I call

The Basic Blues Brush

Finger an E chord.

The basic underlying rhythmic feeling of blues is a pulsating series of long-short, long-short beats. In this series the "long" is twice as long as the "short." This would be, in a sense, equivalent to our "bass-chord" $\frac{6}{8}$ strum.

This rhythmic figure may be executed in a number of ways on the guitar. We will first use down-up brush strokes: The first beat ("long") is a downstroke with the thumb; the second beat ("short") is an upstroke with the index finger.

The metrical feeling of blues is, however, not $\frac{6}{8}$, but $\frac{4}{4}$. There are four "down-ups" per measure. In order to make this add up to four beats we must introduce a new musical symbol: the triplet sign. This is gone into in greater detail in

the section on note reading (Section Eight). As far as we are concerned here, there is no difference in the actual sound of these rhythmic figures (with or without the triplet sign).

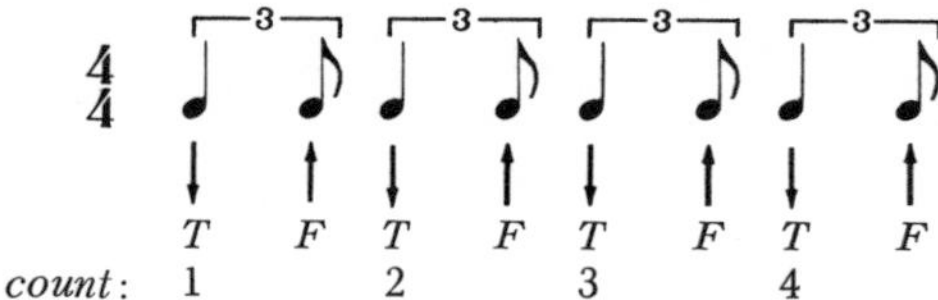

Try it with A and B7.

The Blue Note

Harmonically, one of the most important characteristics of blues is the blurring of the line between major and minor. This harmonic blurring is a reflection of a comparable vocal ambiguity. To put it in terms of the guitar—the alternate playing of a major and minor chord with the same root (e.g. E major and E minor) would suggest a blues feeling immediately. Try this alternation in the basic blues brush: one "down-up" for E, one "down-up" for Em . . . and repeat.

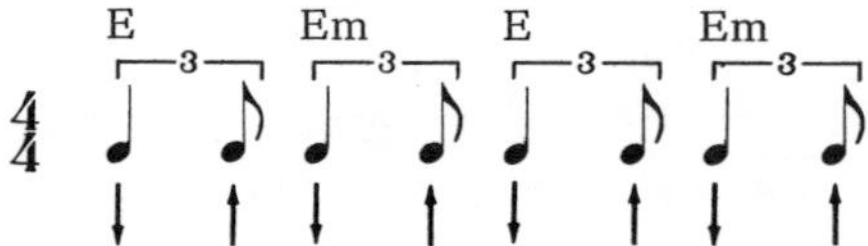

To introduce this blue-note alternation into the A chord we must use a different fingering for the A chord.

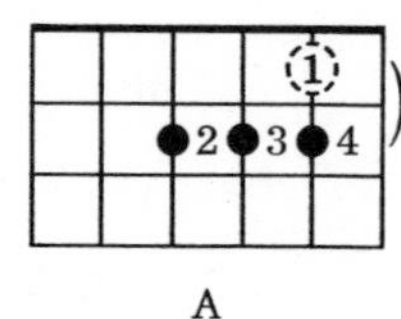

This new fingering makes for an easy shift between A major and A minor.

A Am A Am

For B7, it is the index finger which must be raised to give us the minor feeling. (Incidentally, there's a new chord for you: B minor7.)

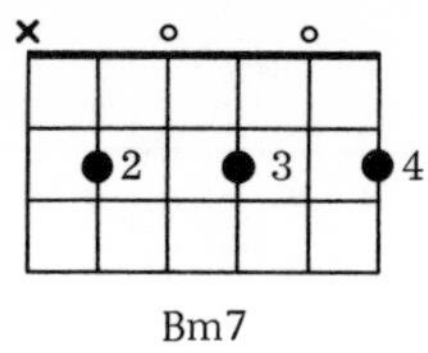

Bm7

Now try *Bricks in My Pillow* using the basic blues brush and the blue-note alternation.

Bricks in My Pillow

Guitar rhythm:

E Em E Em | E Em E Em

I've got

continue rhythm

E Em E Em | E Em E Em | E Em E Em

bricks in my pil - low and my head can't rest no more.

E Em E7 E7 | A Am A Am | A Am A Am

I've got bricks in my pil - low and my head can't rest no

E Em E Em | E Em E Em | B7 Bm7 B7 Bm7

more. Spi - ders crawl - in' on my walls, black snakes

A Am A Am | E Em A Am | 1. E Em B7 | 2. E Em E7

ly - ing on my floor. I've got

E Em E Em E Em E Em E Em E Em E Em E7
I've got mud in my water, I've got drugs all in my tea,
E7 A Am A Am A Am A Am E Em E Em E Em E
I've got mud in my water, I've got drugs all in my tea,
Em B7 Bm7 B7 Bm7 A Am A Am E Em A Am E Em B7
I've got bugs in my beer, and they keep on biting me.

E Em E Em E Em E Em E Em E Em E Em E7
I've got grounds in my coffee, big boll weevil in my meal,
E7 A Am A Am A Am A Am E Em E Em E Em E
I've got grounds in my coffee, big boll weevil in my meal,
Em B7 Bm7 B7 Bm7 A Am A Am E Em A Am E Em B7
I've got tacks in my shoes, keep on stickin' me in the heel.

E Em E Em E Em E Em E Em E Em E Em E7
I've got holes in my pockets, great big patches in my pants,
E7 A Am A Am A Am A Am E Em E Em E Em E
I've got holes in my pockets, great big patches in my pants,
Em B7 Bm7 B7 Bm7 A Am A Am E Em A Am E Em B7
I'm behind with my house rent, landlord wants it in advance.

E Em E Em E Em E Em E Em E Em E Em E7
Well, I feel like walkin' and I feel like lyin' down,
E7 A Am A Am A Am A Am E Em E Em E Em E
Well, I feel like walkin' and I feel like lyin' down,
Em B7 Bm7 B7 Bm7 A Am A Am E Em A Am E Em B7
Well, I feel like drinkin', but there ain't no whisky 'round.

E Em E Em E Em E Em E Em E Em E Em E7
When you hear that bell ringin' and you hear that whistle blow,
E7 A Am A Am A Am A Am E Em E Em E Em E
When you hear that bell ringin' and you hear that whistle blow,
Em B7 Bm7 B7 Bm7 A Am A Am E Em A Am E Em E7
Well, I feel like leavin' but I don't know where to go.

Blues Bass Runs

The bass runs serves much the same function in blues as it does in other types of folk songs: It connects chords. The notes of the runs follow the rhythmic feeling of the accompaniment.

The following song has the bass runs written in in the guitar part. Continue using the blues brush and the blue-note alternation.

Easy Rider

E Em E Em E Em E Em E Em E Em
Eas - y ri-der, just see what you have
Guitar:
continue
E7 Em7 E7 Em7 E7 Em E7 A Am A Am
done, Oh, Lord,
Eas - y ri-der, just
A Am A Am E Em E Em E Em E
see what you have done.
Well, you
A Am A Am A Am A E Em E Em
made me love you, now your gal has come.
E Em E Em E Em E C7 C7 B7 B7
Well, it's hey, hey, hey, hey,

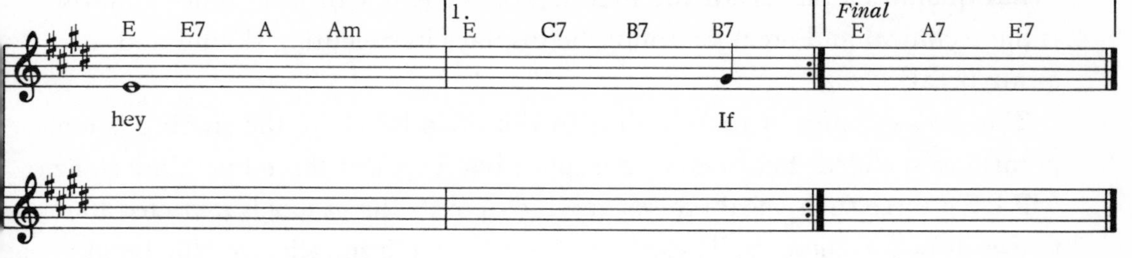

E Em E Em E Em E Em E7 Em7 E7 Em7 E7 Em7 E7 *run*
If I was a catfish, swimmin' in the deep blue sea, Oh Lord,
A Am A Am A Am A Am E Em E Em E Em E
If I was a catfish, swimmin' in the deep blue sea,
run A Am A Am A Am A *run* E Em E Em E Em E
I would swim across the ocean, bring my baby back to me.
Em E Em E *run* C7 C7 B7 B7 E E7 A Am E C7 B7 B7
Well, it's hey, hey, hey, hey, hey.

E Em E Em E Em E Em E7 Em7 E7 Em7 E7 Em7 E7 *run*
I'm goin' away, Rider, and I won't be back till fall, Oh, Lord,
A Am A Am A Am A Am E Em E Em E Em E
I'm goin' away, Rider, and I won't be back till fall,
run A Am A Am A Am A *run* E Em E Em E Em E
And if I find me a good man, I won't be back at all.
Em E Em E *run* C7 C7 B7 B7 E E7 A Am E A7 E7
Well, it's hey, hey, hey, hey, hey.

Blues Arpeggios

The same rhythm, as played with the blues brush, may be played in arpeggio style. Play the following pattern with a C chord.

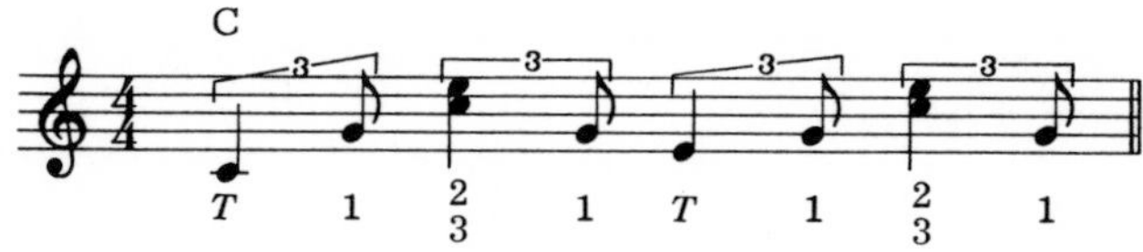

The Break

The blues guitarist really comes into his own when he starts playing instrumental breaks (or interludes) in his accompaniments. Blues guitar playing at its most typical best is essentially a duet, or dialogue, between voice and guitar.

What qualifies a player for the high honor of being called a "blues guitarist" is the technical and creative ability he displays in executing skillful and interesting breaks.

The break comes at those points in the melody where the singing is temporarily suspended. Because of blues phrasing a typical three-line blues stanza will have three such vocal pauses at which points the guitar is expected to interject its own comments. These "comments"—the inspiration for the breaks—may, at the beginning of study (and, for that matter, at any other time), be drawn from the vocal melodic material.

Follow the guitar part closely in the next two songs. Use the blues arpeggio.

Shuckin' Sugar Blues

C

I've got your pic - ture

Guitar: *continue*

and I'm gon - na put it in a frame.

C7 F

I've got your pic - ture and I'm gon - na put it

C
in a frame, Shuck - in' su - gar
And then if you leave home we can find you just the
G7
F(7)
C
F(7)
same.
1. C
G7
Final
C

C   C *break* C7
Now, if you don't love me, please don't dog me 'round,
        F   C   *break*
If you don't love me, please don't dog me 'round—Shuckin' sugar—
      G7   F(7)   C F(7) *break* C G7
If you dog me 'round I know you'll put me down.

C   C *break* C7
Oh, say, Sarah Brown, somethin's gone on wrong,
F   C   *break*
Say, Sarah Brown, somethin's done gone wrong—Shuckin' sugar—
G7   F(7)   C F(7) *break* C G7
The woman I love, she done been here and gone.

C   C *break* C7
Oh, listen, Sarah Brown, don't you want to go?
F   C   *break*
Oh, Sarah Brown, don't you want to go?—Shuckin' sugar—
G7   F(7)   C F(7) *break* C G7
Want to take you 'cross the water where that brown-skin man can't go.

C C *break* C7
I am worried here, and I'm worried everywhere,
F C *break*
I am worried here, and I'm worried everywhere—Shuckin' sugar—
G7 F(7) C F(7) *break* C G7
Man, I stretched out at home, and I'll not be worried there

C C *break* C7
I'm tired of marryin', tired of this settlin' down.
F C *break*
Tired of bein' married, tired of this settlin' down—Shuckin' sugar—
G7 F(7) C F(7) *break* C
I only want to stay like I am and slip from town to town.

Broke and Hungry

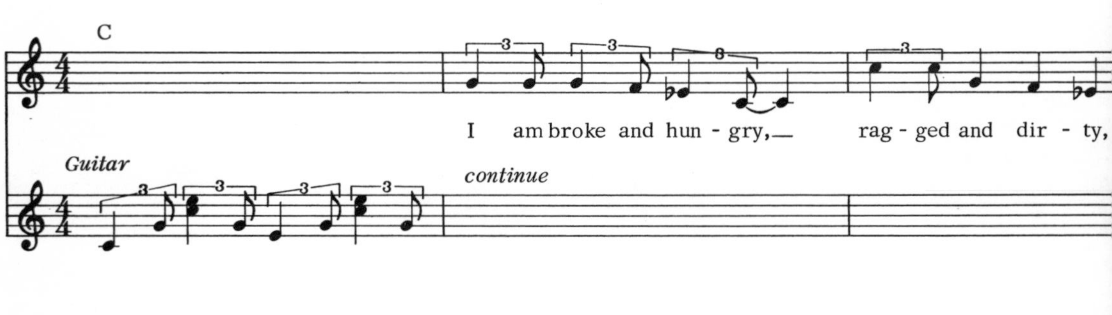

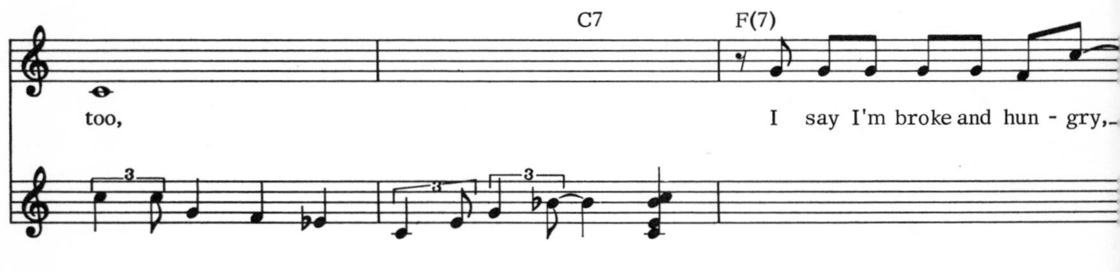

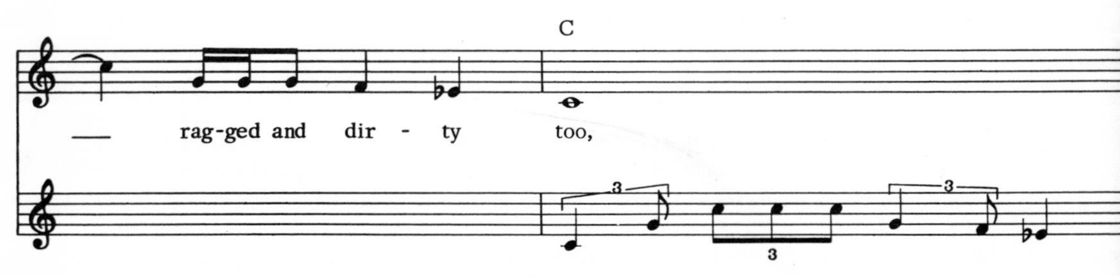

G7
F(7)
Ma - ma, if I clean up can I go home with
C
F(7)
1.
C
G7
Final
C
C7
you?

C   break C7
I am motherless, fatherless, sister- and brotherless too,
F(7)   C break
I say I'm motherless, fatherless, sister- and brotherless too,
G7   F(7)   C F(7) C G7
Reason I tried so hard to make this trip with you.

C   break C7
You miss me, woman, count the days I'm gone.
F(7)   C break
You miss me, woman, count the days I'm gone.
G7   F(7)   C F(7) C G7
I'm goin' away to build me a railroad of my own.

C   break C7
I feel like jumpin' through the keyhole in your door,
F(7)   C break
I feel like jumpin' through the keyhole in your door,
G7   F(7)   C F(7) C G7
If you jump this time, baby, you won't jump no more.

C   break C7
I believe my good gal has found my black cat bone,
F(7)   C break
I say, I b'lieve my good gal has found my black cat bone.
G7   F(7)   C F(7) C G7
I can leave Sunday morning; Monday morning I'm stickin' 'round home.

C   break C7
I want to show you women what careless love has done,
F(7)   C break
I want to show you women what careless love has done,
G7   F(7)   C F(7) C C7
Caused a man like me to be a great long way from home.

The Chord Slide

When it comes to expanding your instrumental horizons you will observe that all keys are not created equal. The major-minor blue-note alternation, for example, so easily accomplished with E and A, would be rather difficult with C or G. Each key has "a little something" that sets it apart from the others by virtue of the nature of the tuning of the guitar.

The "ultimate" in blue-note *alternation* would be achieved by playing an entire chord one fret lower than normal and then sliding it back to its proper fret. This is most gracefully accomplished with D.

Finger what looks like a D chord—but at the first and second frets.

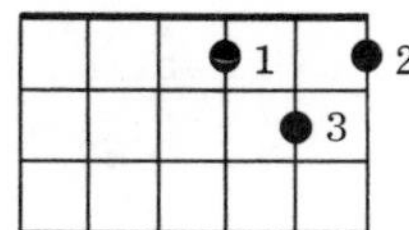

Play the first four strings by brushing down with your thumb—and while they are still sounding slide back up to D.

Here is another very common fingering for A7 which then may be slid from one fret lower as with the D.

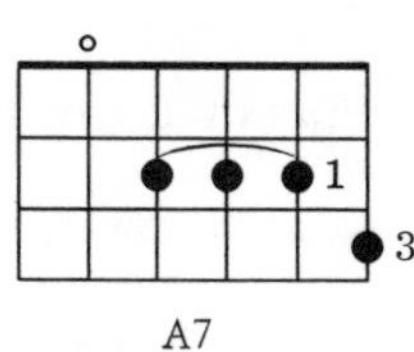

We would incorporate these chords into the blues brush in the following manner: the lowered chords (D-flat, A-flat7) on the fourth and eighth beats of this strum (they are the second and fourth *upstrokes* of the sequence).

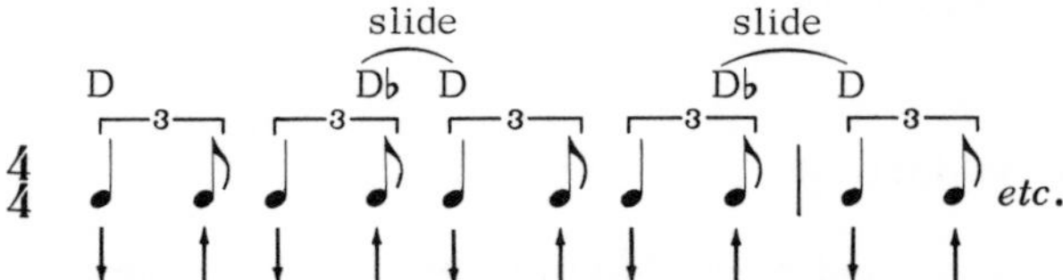

Look for these slides in *High-Price Blues*. See what you can do with the breaks as well.

High-Price Blues

D♭ D   D♭   D   D♭ D   D♭ D
Walked in a meat market   just about   noon,
D♭ D   D♭   D   Ddim7   D7   Ddim7 D7
Hear them hollerin', "Now the cow jumped over the moon." *Chorus*

D♭ D   D♭ D   D♭ D   D♭ D
Johnny's gone to war, Jimmy's gone to sea,
D♭ D   D♭   D   Ddim7 D7   Ddim7 D7
But I tell you high prices is   killin'   me. *Chorus*

D♭ D   D♭   D   D♭ D   D♭ D
Meat, butter, and eggs   gettin' higher still,
D♭ D   D♭ D   Ddim7 D7   Ddim7 D7
You don't even get no change out of a   five-dollar   bill.

Chorus:

G7   D♭ D
Prices goin' higher; yes 'way up higher,
      A♭7 A7   A♭7 A7
Well, it's no disgrace to be poor,
      G7   D♭ D G7 D A7
But it's a little unhandy for me.

D♭ D   D♭ D   D♭ D   D♭ D
The horses and the numbers—odds are still the same,
D♭ D   D♭ D   Ddim7 D7   Ddim7 D7
Looks like the prices would raise ten percent on the game.

Chorus:

G7   D♭ D
Prices goin' higher; yes, 'way up higher,
       A♭7 A7   A♭7 A7
Prices goin' so high,
 G7   D♭ D G7 D
I don't think I will work no more.

Stop-Rhythm

Knowing when not to play is as important as knowing when and how to play. In certain situations emphasis is gained by playing sharply on, say, the first beat of a measure and then not playing for the rest of the measure. This process may be repeated for a number of measures. The chord, once struck, may be allowed to sound for the whole measure—or, often, it may be muffled almost immediately after it has been played. This muffling produces an interesting and characteristic percussive effect. The muffling may be done with the palm or the heel of the right hand.

Play an E chord with a series of rapid downstrokes and muffle the chord after each beat.

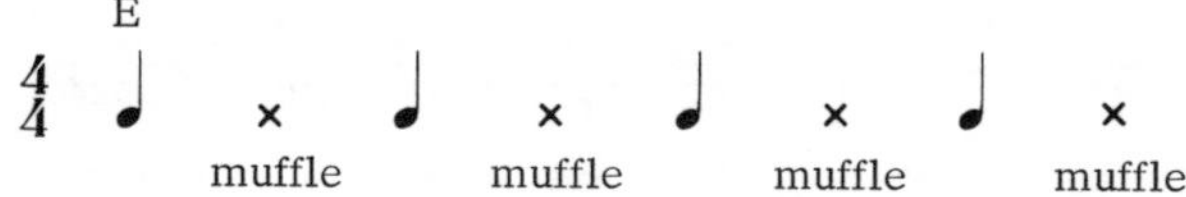

Play a series of blues brushes with similar muffling.

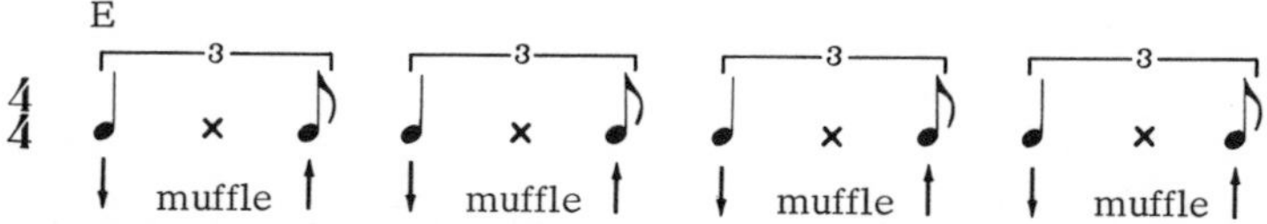

Play the same series of brushes but make each upstroke an E minor chord (blue-note alternation). Muffle after each downstroke.

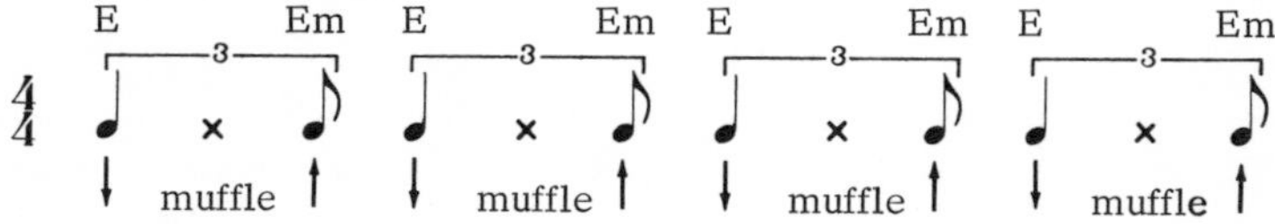

Play only the following parts of this sequence: the last beat (the upstroke on E minor) and the first beat (the downstroke on E).

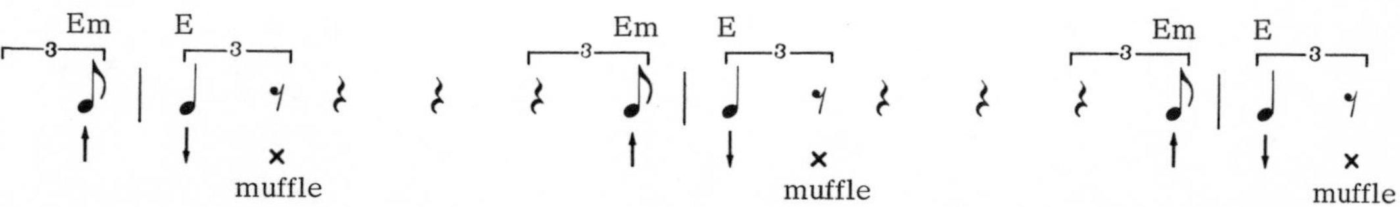

Use this technique in the first part of *Evil-Hearted Man.*

Evil-Hearted Man

Guitar

Em
When the

E Em
sun rose this morn - in' I was

E Em
feel - in' might - y bad, My

E Em
ba - by said, "Good morn - ing," Hell, it

E7
made me mad;

Chorus
Be - cause I was

A7
e - vil,

E - vil-heart-ed

E
me.

continue

B7
A7
I'm just down-right e-vil, E-vil as a man can
Blues brush

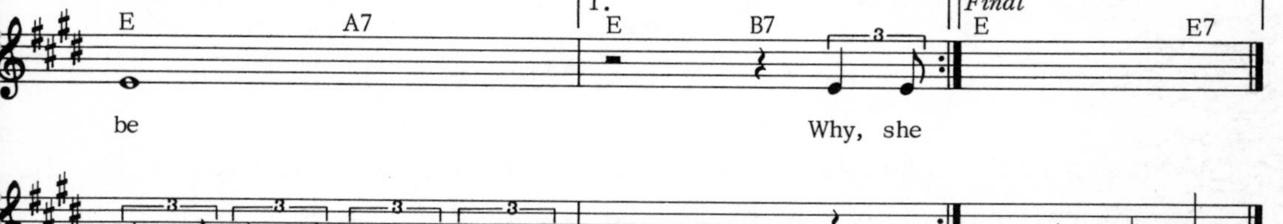
E
A7
1.
E
B7
Final
E
E7
be
Why, she

Em E
Why, she even cooked my breakfast,
Em E
And she brought it to my bed,
Em E
I took a sip of coffee,
Em E7
Throwed the cup at her head. *Chorus*

Em E
I've sold out to the devil,
Em E
Trouble's all I crave.
Em E
I'd like to see you dead
Em E7
And lying in your grave. *Chorus*

Em E
I don't even care
Em E
If it rains from now on,
Em E
And the gal I love
Em E7
Had never been born. *Chorus*

Em E
I don't care
Em E
If my baby leaves me flat,
Em E
I've got forty 'leven others
Em E7
If it comes to that. *Chorus*

A Little Blues Picking

One of the most effective guitar blues techniques involves the thumb maintaining a steady beat of the bass note or notes of a chord while the fingers play some rhythmic-melodic pattern on the higher strings.

Finger this altered G chord.

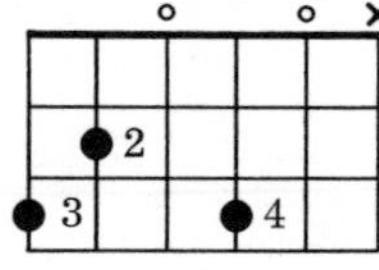

Start a slow, steady beat going with the thumb over the bass strings. It doesn't matter precisely how many strings your thumb strikes—two or three.

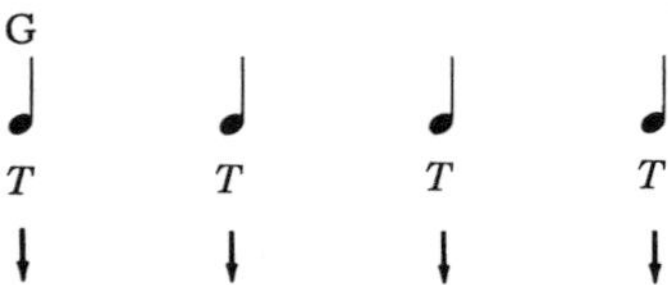

Add the following pattern on the second and third strings with the first and second fingers while the thumb continues on the bass.

Finger C7 in this manner
and keep the same pattern going.

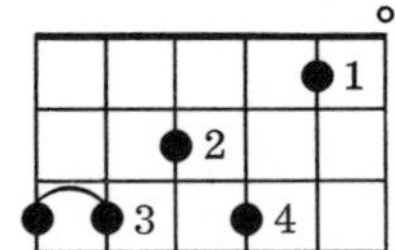

Baby, Please Don't Go

G
Babe, I'm way down here,
C7
You know, I'm way down here,
G
Babe, I'm way down here in a rollin' fog,
D7 G
Baby, please don't go.

G
Baby, please don't go,
C7
Baby, please don't go,
G
Baby, please don't go back to New Orleans,
D7 G
You know it hurts me so.

G
Babe, I'm way down here,
C7
You know, I'm way down here,
G
Babe, I'm way down here on old Parchman Farm,
D7 G
Baby, please don't go.

G
Baby, please don't go,
C7
Baby, please don't go,
G
Baby, please don't go and leave me here,
D7 G
You know it's cold down here.

G
Babe, I'm way down here,
C7
You know, I'm way down here,
G
Babe, I'm way down here on old Parchman Farm,
D7 G
Baby, please don't go.

G
You know, it's cold down here,
C7
Babe, it's cold down here,
G
You know, it's cold down here on old Parchman Farm,
D7 G
Baby, please don't go.

G
Baby, please don't go,
C7
Baby, please don't go,
G
Baby, please don't go and leave me here,
D7 G
You know it's cold down here.

G
I'm half dead down here,
C7
I'm half dead down here,
G
I'm half dead down here on old Parchman Farm,
D7 G
Baby, please don't go.

If we want to play in this style in the key of C we must play F in such a way as to give us the necessary bass notes. This introduces a new concept in the playing of chords: the *barre* ("bar").

Lay the first finger of the left hand *flat* across all the strings at the first fret. Press down hard on the side of your finger (the side nearest the thumb) and play all six strings. You will probably not get a clear tone on all strings immediately. This will take some experimenting with finger positions—and practice.

With the remaining three fingers play what would be an E chord if the guitar fingerboard began at your index finger.

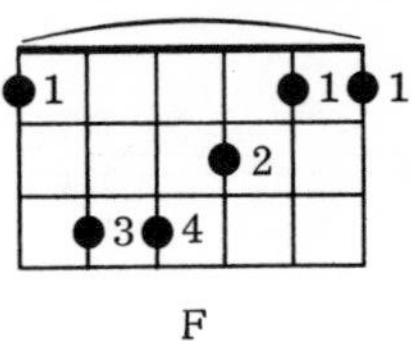

Try some of your old songs in C with F played this way.

Now, reach with your left pinky to the fourth fret (I'm not kidding). This is a very important chord.

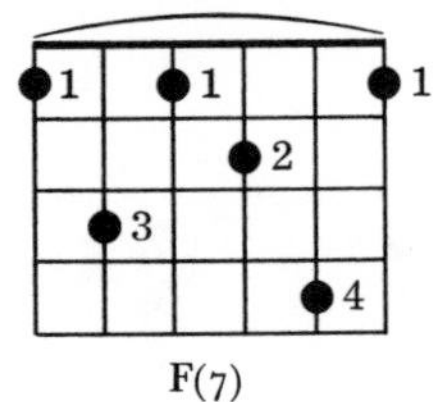

It may help you to play an altered C chord this way first.

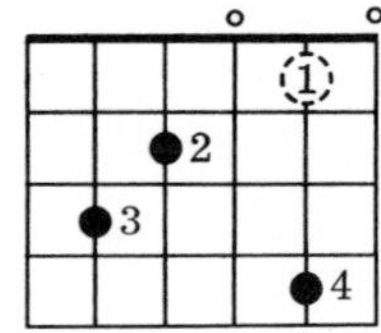

Using this C chord, play the following picking pattern.

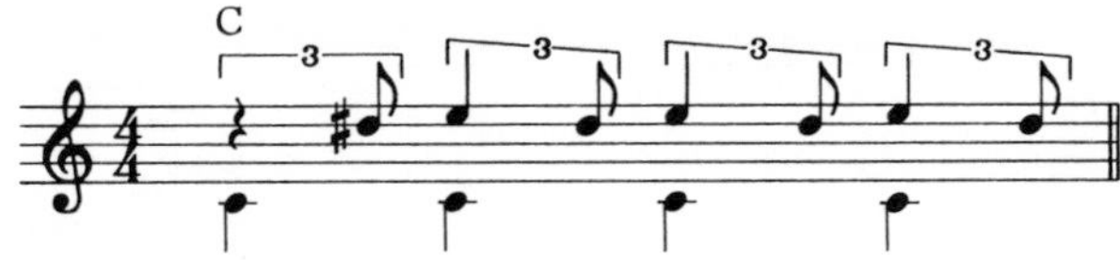

Now that your pinky has been somewhat strengthened (if it hasn't already fallen off) try the following pattern with F(7).

Shorty George combines these patterns with some other breaks.

Shorty George

C
Guitar:
Oh, well - a Short - y George
he ain't no friend of mine,
C7
Oh, well - a
F(7)
Short - y George he ain't no friend of
C
mine,
He's tak - en all the wo-men and left the men be -
G7
Blues brush

C C C7
Shorty George, he done been here and gone,
F(7) C
Yes, Shorty George, he done been here and gone,
G7 C F(7) C G7
Lord, he left many a poor man a great long way from home.

C C C7
My mama died when I was a lad,
F(7) C
My mama died when I was a lad,
G7 C F(7) C G7
And ever since I been to the bad.

C C C7
Well, my babe caught the Katy, I caught the Santa Fe(e),
F(7) C
Well, she caught the Katy and I caught the Santa Fe(e),
G7 C F(7) C G7
Well, you can't quit me, baby, can't you see?

C C C7
Well, I went to Galveston—work on the Mallory Line,
F(7) C
Went to Galveston—Lord, on the Mallory Line,
G7 C F(7) C G7
Babe, you can't quit me—ain't no use tryin'.

C C C7
Shorty George, travelin' through the land,
F(7) C
Shorty George, he's travelin' through the land,
G7 C F(7) C G7
Always lookin' to pick some poor woman's man.

C C C7
When I get back to Dallas, I'm gonna walk and tell,
F(7) C
When I get back to Dallas, gonna walk and tell,
G7 C F(7) C G7
That the Fort Bend bottom is a burning hell.

Repeat Verse One

Here is a useful fingering for the A chord.

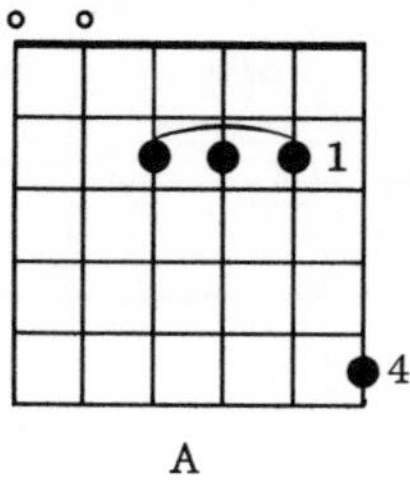
1
4
A

Using this "long" A chord we can develop some interesting variations between it and A7.

A

One of the vocal characteristics of blues is the occasional use of the falsetto—a sort of thin, yodel-like vocal quality. *Prison Bound,* here written in a key that may seem high to many, would be very effectively sung if falsetto were utilized at certain high points. Follow the accompaniment closely.

Prison Bound

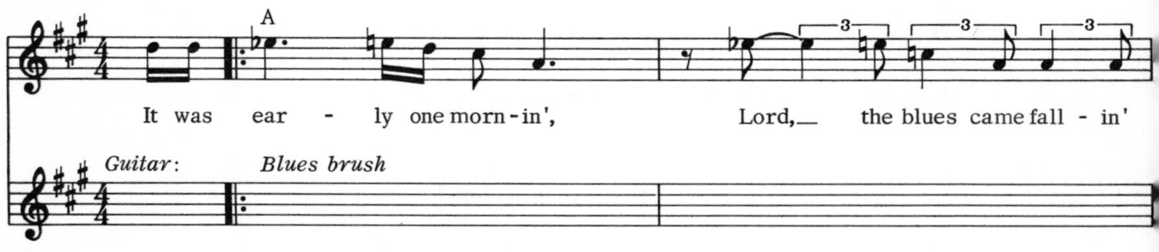
A
It was ear - ly one morn - in', Lord,__ the blues came fall - in'
Guitar:
Blues brush

A7
D7
down. It was ear - ly one morn-in', the
Blues brush

A
blues came fall - in' down. I'm
E7
D7
all locked up in jail, Lord, and I'm pris - on
Blues brush
A D
1. A E7
Final A
bound. It was

A A A7
It was all last night I sat in my cell and moaned,
D7 A
It was all last night I sat in my cell and moaned,
E7 D7 A D7 A E7
Thinkin' about my baby, great God, and my happy home.

A A A7
Now, baby, you will never see my smilin' face again,
D7 A
Now, baby, you will never see my smilin' face again,
E7 D7 A D7 A E7
But you always can remember that your daddy has been your friend.

A A A7
At my trial, baby, you could not be found,
D7 A
At my trial, baby, you could not be found;
E7 D7 A D7 A
It's too late, mistreatin' woman, you know I'm prison bound.

SECTION SEVEN

CALYPSO AND LATIN RHYTHMS

Syncopation

The music of the West Indies and other Caribbean Islands possesses, among other things, a relative degree of rhythmic complexity not found in the folk music of the northern latitudes. This complexity has a name: *syncopation.* Syncopation is the effect caused by the misplacing of rhythmic accents—by the interchanging of weak and strong beats—by putting the ac*cent* on the wrong syl*lable.* This may be done in a variety of ways.

Play a C chord.

Ordinarily in a measure of $\frac{4}{4}$ there will be four accents per measure—with the first and third beats being, perhaps, somewhat emphasized.

1 2 3 4

If we subdivide the four quarter notes into eight eighth notes (as we do when we play arpeggios) the basic displacement of pulses is not significantly altered.

But what happens if we group these eight eighth notes not into four groups of two (or two groups of four), but into three groups of three, three, and two beats each, respectively?

If we play the first eighth note of each group with the thumb and follow with an arpeggio with the first and second fingers for the second and third, fifth and sixth, and eighth (just the first finger here) we have a first-class syncopated rhythm. This comes about because the thumb on the bass naturally produces a heavier accent than a finger playing an arpeggio.

Play this pattern with the thumb alternating from fifth (A) to fourth (D) to third (G) string and with the first two fingers playing the arpeggio on the first two strings.

Try the same thing with G7. Here the thumb plays strings 6, 5, and 4. The first two fingers may remain on the first two strings, or, if you like, you may experiment with different string combinations.

With F, the thumb plays 4, 3, and 2 and the last eighth note is played by the second finger on the first string.

Hey Lolly, Lolly Lo

C
Married men will keep your secret,
G7
Hey lolly, lolly lo.

Single boys will talk about you,
C
Hey lolly, lolly lo. *Chorus*

C
I have a girl, she's ten feet tall,
G7
Hey lolly, lolly lo.

Sleeps in the kitchen with her feet in the hall,
C
Hey lolly, lolly lo. *Chorus*

C
Two old maids a-sittin' in the sand,
G7
Hey lolly, lolly lo.
Each one wishin' that the other was a man,
C
Hey lolly, lolly lo. *Chorus*

C
Everybody sing the chorus,
G7
Hey lolly, lolly lo,
Either you're against us or you're for us,
C
Hey lolly, lolly lo. *Chorus*

C
The purpose of this little song,
G7
Hey lolly, lolly lo.
Is to make up verses as you go along,
C
Hey lolly, lolly lo. *Chorus*

Everybody Loves Saturday Night

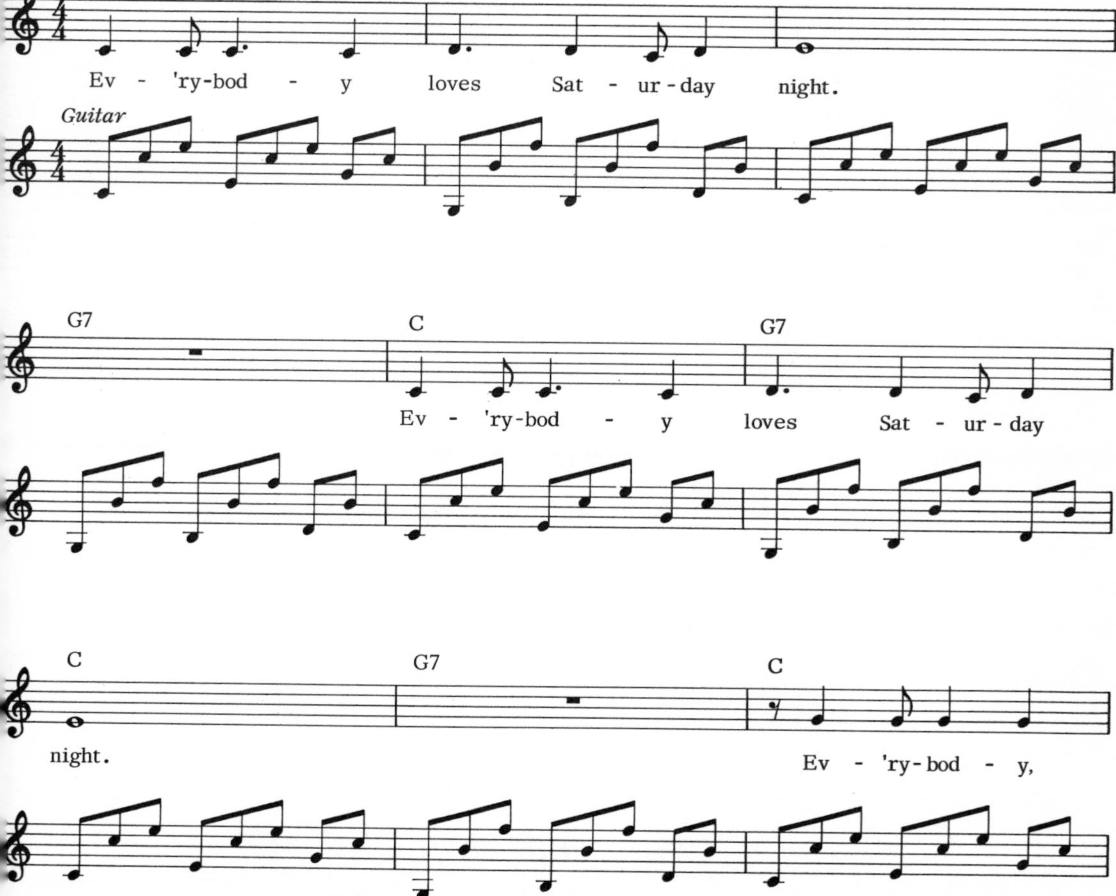

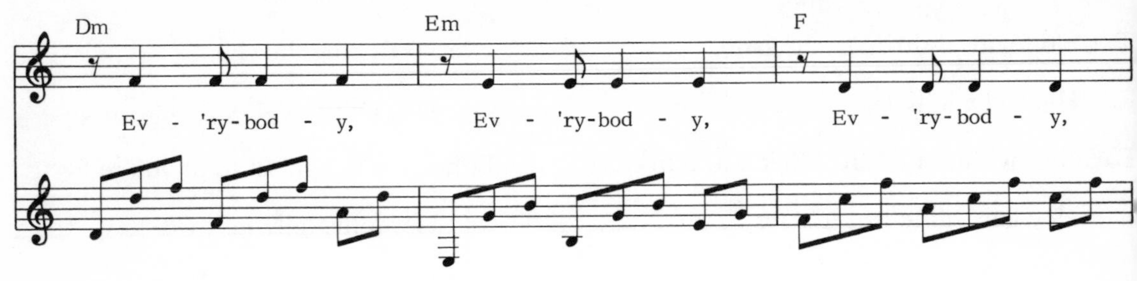

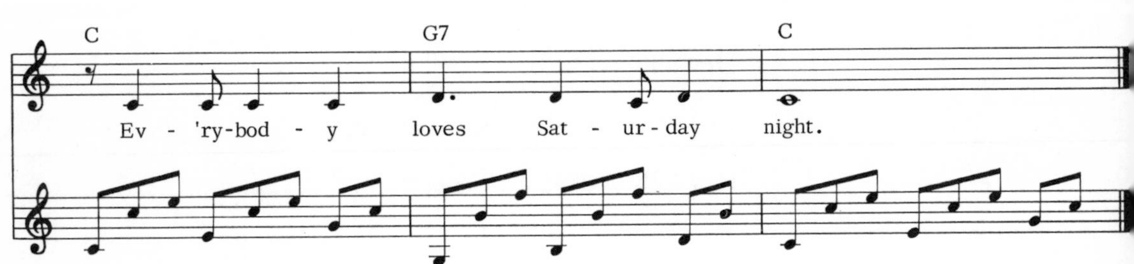

Nigerian: (original language)

C G7 C
Bobo waro fero Satodeh,
G7 C
Bobo waro fero Satodeh.
Dm
Bobo waro, bobo waro,
Em F
Bobo waro, bobo waro,
C G7 C
Bobo waro fero Satodeh.

French:

C G7 C
Tout le monde aime Samedi soir,
G7 C
Tout le monde aime Samedi soir.
Dm
Tout le monde, tout le monde,
Em F
Tout le monde, tout le monde,
C G7 C
Tout le monde aime Samedi soir.

Yiddish:

C G7 C
Yeder eyner hot lieb Shabas ba nacht,
G7 C
Yeder eyner hot lieb Shabas ba nacht.
Dm
Yeder eyner, yeder eyner,
Em F
Yeder eyner, yeder eyner,
C G7 C
Yeder eyner hot lieb Shabas ba nacht.

C G7 C
Chinese: Ren ren si huan li pai lu,
G7 C
Ren ren si huan li pai lu.
Dm
Ren ren si, ren ren si,
Em F
Ren ren si, ren ren si,
C G7 C
Ren ren si huan li pai lu.

C G7 C
Russian: Fsiem nravitsa subbota vietcher,
G7 C
Fsiem nravitsa subbota vietcher.
Dm
Fsiem nravitsa, fsiem nravitsa,
Em F
Fsiem nravitsa, fsiem nravitsa,
C G7 C
Fsiem nravitsa subbota vietcher.

C G7 C
Czech: Kazhdi ma rad sabotu vietcher,
G7 C
Kazhdi ma rad sabotu vietcher.
Dm
Kazhdi ma, kazhdi ma,
Em F
Kazhdi ma, kazhdi ma,
C G7 C
Kazhdi ma rad sabotu vietcher.

C G7 C
Spanish: A todos le gusta la noche del Sabado,
G7 C
A todos le gusta la noche del Sabado.
Dm
A todos le gusta, a todos le gusta,
Em F
A todos le gusta, a todos le gusta,
C G7 C
A todos le gusta la noche del Sabado.

C G7 C
Ertruscan: All the cats dig Saturday night the most,
G7 C
All the cats dig Saturday night the most.
Dm
All the cats, all the cats,
Em F
All the cats, all the cats,
C G7 C
All the cats dig Saturday night the most.

Play an E chord.
Play a series of eight unsyncopated down-up strokes.

Now do not play the fifth eighth note (the downstroke). In effect you are tying the fourth and fifth eighth notes together.

This is another kind of syncopation. We have eliminated a downbeat.

In this next song there are three points at which the chord changes in the "middle" of the strum. The change actually takes place on the fourth eighth note (upstroke). Don't let the chord change affect the rhythm—just keep going.

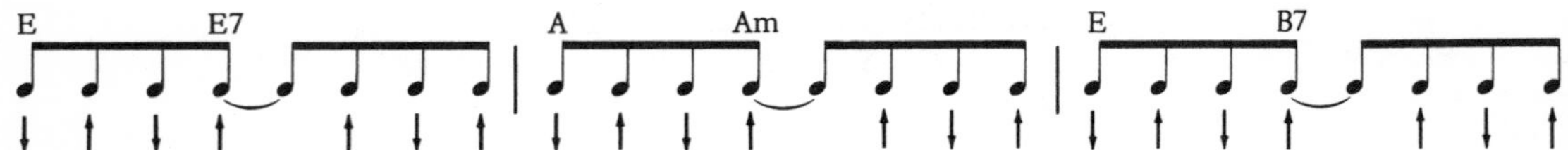

Run Come See Jerusalem

E
That day they were talking 'bout a storm in the islands,
B7
Run come see, run come see.
E E7 A
They were talking 'bout a storm in the islands,
Am E B7 E
Run come see Jerusalem.

E
That day there were three ships leaving out the harbor,
B7
Run come see, run come see.
E E7 A
There were three ships leaving out the harbor,
Am E B7 E
Run come see Jerusalem.

E
It was the Ethel, the Myrtle and the Pretoria,
B7
Run come see, run come see.
E E7 A
The Ethel, the Myrtle and Pretoria,
Am E B7 E
Run come see Jerusalem.

E
They were bound for the Island of Andros,
B7
Run come see, run come see.
E E7 A
They were bound for the Island of Andros,
Am E B7 E
Run come see Jerusalem.

E
The Pretoria was out on the ocean,
B7
Run come see, run come see.
E E7 A
The Pretoria was out on the ocean,
Am E B7 E
Run come see Jerusalem.

E
Right then it was a big sea built up in the northwest,
B7
Run come see, run come see.
E E7 A
Then a big sea built up in the northwest,
Am E B7 E
Run come see Jerusalem.

E
My God, when the first wave hit the Pretoria,
B7
Run come see, run come see.
E E7 A
When the first wave hit the Pretoria,
Am E B7 E
Run come see Jerusalem.

E
My God, there were thirty-three souls on the water,
B7
Run come see, run come see.
E E7 A
There were thirty-three souls on the water,
Am E B7 E
Run come see Jerusalem.

E
My God, now, George Brown he was the captain,
B7
Run come see, run come see.
E E7 A
George Brown he was the captain,
Am E B7 E
Run come see Jerusalem.

E
He said, "Come now, witness your judgment."
B7
Run come see, run come see.
E E7 A
He said, "Come now, witness your judgment."
Am E B7 E
Run come see Jerusalem.

E
There'll be no more waiting on Andros,
B7
Run come see, run come see.
E E7 A
There'll be no more waiting on Andros,
Am E B7 E
Run come see Jerusalem.

In *'Round the Bay of Mexico* there are quite a few syncopated chord changes.

'Round the Bay of Mexico

C
Vhen I was a young man in my prime,
F C
Way oh, Susianna!
F Em Dm G7
'd love those pretty girls two at a time,
C Dm G7 C
'Round the Bay of Mexico. *Chorus*

C
The reason those girls they love me so,
F C
Way oh, Susianna!
F Em Dm G7
Because I don't tell everything that I know,
C Dm G7 C
'Round the Bay of Mexico. *Chorus*

C
Them Nassau girls ain't got no combs,
F C
Way oh, Susianna!
F Em Dm G7
They comb their hair with whipper-back bones,
C Dm G7 C
'Round the Bay of Mexico. *Chorus*

Another important aspect of music of the Caribbean is the percussive quality of some of its guitar accompaniments.

Play an E chord.

Play a downstroke with your thumb. Then, with your fingers loosely clenched in a semi fist, strike the strings with your knuckles over the point where the fingerboard meets the sound hole. You should hear the sound of the strings clicking against the metal frets.

Try two eighth-note down-up strokes and two eighth-note knucks.

Try various patterns.

The famous Cuban song *Guantanamera* is here written with a two-guitar accompaniment. One accompaniment is this new percussive one, the other is a syncopated melodic one. Invite a friend over.

Guantanamera

B7
Verse
E
A
B7
ra. Yo soy un hom - bre sin - ce - ro, de don - de
E
A
B7
E
A
cre - ce lo pal - ma, Yo soy un hom - bre sin - ce - ro,
B7
E
A
B7
de don - de cre - - ce la pal - ma, Y an - tes de
E
A
B7
E
A
B7
mo - rir me quie - - ro E - char - mis ver - sos del al - ma.

Mi verso es de un verde claro,
Y de un carmin encendido.
Mi verso es de un verde claro,
Y de un carmin encendido.
Mi verso es un cierro herido,
Que busca en el monte amparo. *Chorus*

Con los pobres de la tierra
Quiero yo mi suerte echar.
Con los pobres de la tierra
Quiero yo mi suerte echar.
El arroyo de la sierra
Me complace mas que el mar. *Chorus*

English translation:

A truthful man, that's me;
From where the palm trees grow.
Before I die, I'd like to
Pour forth the verses of my soul.

My verse is bright green,
And also flowing carmine.
My verse is a wounded fawn
Seeking refuge in the woods.

With the poor of the earth
I want to share my fate.
The mountain brook
Pleases me more than the sea.

The Chilean folksong *Mi Caballo Blanco* is one of many South American songs in triple meter where there is a syncopation involving shifting accents within the measure.

The six eighth notes that make up each measure may be thought of as three groups of two

Em
3/4
T chord T ch T ch

or two groups of three.

Try the following changing pattern.

Don't change the *tempo* from measure to measure. Do follow the accents as laid down by the thumb.

Mi Caballo Blanco

(My White Horse)

Em Am
En alas de una dicha
B7 Em
Mi caballo corrió,
Am Em
Y en brazos de una pena
B7 Em
También él me llevó. *Chorus*

Em Am
Hasta que a Dios le pido
B7 Em
Que lo tenga muy bien,
Am Em
Si a su lado me llama,
B7 Em
En mi blanquito iré. *Chorus*

English translation:

My white horse
Is as white as the dawn.
We always travel together,
He is my best friend.

Chorus:
My horse, my horse,
Goes galloping.
My horse, my horse
Goes on and on.

On the wings of happiness
My horse raced on.
And in the arms of sorrow
He bore me, as well.

I even ask the Lord
To keep him safe and sound.
But if he calls me to his side
I'll go on little "Whitey."

Finger an A minor chord.

Strike the fourth string (while playing the chord).

Hammer-on with the pinky on the third fret of the fourth string and follow with a down-up banjo brush.

Try the same hammer (pinky—third fret—fourth string) while playing an E chord.

Now try the following variation.

Another characteristic Spanish "sound" is gotten by playing a melodic passage on the lower strings while "answering back" each note with the open E (first) string.

A song from the Spanish Civil War. If the key is too high for you to sing in comfortably put a capo on the third or fourth fret and sing an octave lower.

Si Me Quieres Escribir

(If You Want To Write To Me)

Am
E
Si me
Guitar:
H H H H
Am
E
quie - res es cri - bir, Ya sa - bes mi pa - ra -
H H H H
Am
E
de - ro
Si me
H
Am
E
quie-res es - cri - bir, Ya sa - bes mi pa - ra -
H H H
Am
G
Am
G
de - ro: En el fren - te de Gan - de - sa, pri - mer - a lin -

Am
Si tu quieres comer bien,
E Am E
Barato y de buena forma,
Am
Si tu quieres comer bien,
E Am
Barato y de buena forma,
G Am
En el frente de Gandesa,
G F E
Allí tienen una fonda.
Am G
En el frente de Gandesa,
F E
Allí tienen una fonda.

Am
En la entrada de la fonda
E Am E
Hay un moro Mojame.
Am
En la entrada de la fonda
E Am
Hay un moro Mojame,
G Am
Que te dice, "Pasa, pasa,
G F E
"Que quieres para comer."
Am G
Que te dice, "Pasa, pasa,
F E
"Que quieres para comer."

Am
El primer plato que dan
E Am
Son grenadas rompedoras
Am
El primer plato que dan
E Am
Son grenadas rompedoras
G Am
El segundo de metralla,
G F E
Para recordar memorias.
Am G
El segundo de metralla,
F E
Para recordar memorias.

Repeat Verse One

English translation:

If you want to write to me
You already know my address.
On the Gandesa front
In the first line of fire.

If you want to eat well,
Cheaply and in good style,
On the Gandesa front
There is an inn.

At the entrance to the inn
There is a Moor, Mohammed,
Who says to enter
If you want to eat.

The first dish they give you
Is hand grenades.
The second is shrapnel,
So you won't forget.

SECTION EIGHT

NOTE READING

The Open Strings

The notation of music is done on the lines and in the spaces of a five-lined system called a staff.

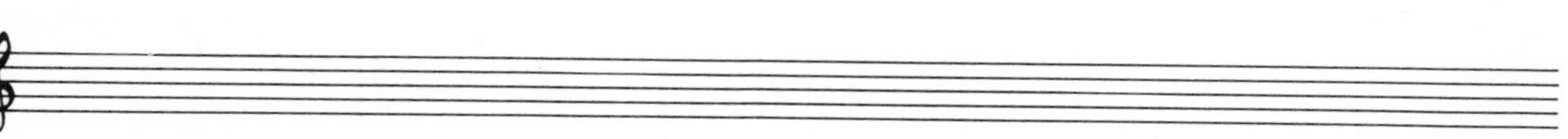

These lines and spaces take on specific note names when we add a *G clef.* The G clef gets its name from its shape and from the fact that its lower loop curves around the G line on the staff.

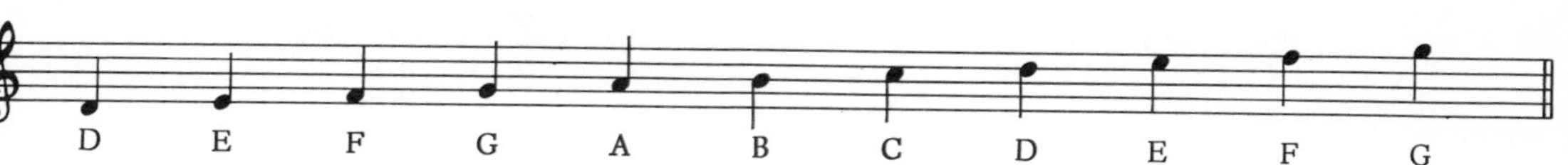

To write notes above or below the staff we use ledger lines. These lines may be thought of as either higher or lower extensions of the original five lines of the staff.

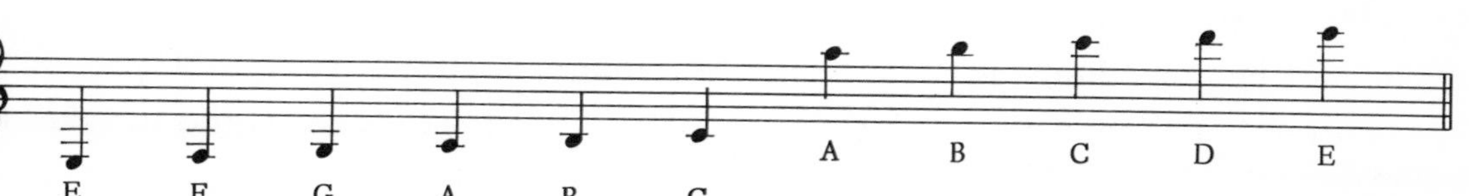

These notes all may be played on the guitar. Among them are the six open strings.

In playing the following Exercises use the thumb for the notes on the sixth, fifth, and fourth strings and the first and second fingers *alternately* for the notes on the third, second, and first strings.

Here is an exercise for the open strings of the guitar.

Rhythm

Up to now we have been concerned only with identifying the six open strings. Before we go any further with the learning of notes we must introduce the concept of rhythm and note value. Without actually saying so we have assumed that all the notes played up to now were played at a steady speed and that each one had the same time duration as another. The kind of note value we have used to express this relationship is the *quarter note.*

The direction of the stem (up or down) does not affect the note value. It is done for purely typographical purposes, to avoid having the stems extend either too far above or too far below the staff.

A quarter note, in and of itself, gives us no indication of how rapidly it should be played or how long it should remain sounding. A series of quarter notes only indicates that, relative to each other, the notes are equal in time. Considerations of speed (that is, tempo) are left up to the performer or composer.

In a piece of music notes are usually grouped together in short segments containing the same number of beats. These segments are called *measures.* Measures are separated from each other by *bar lines.*

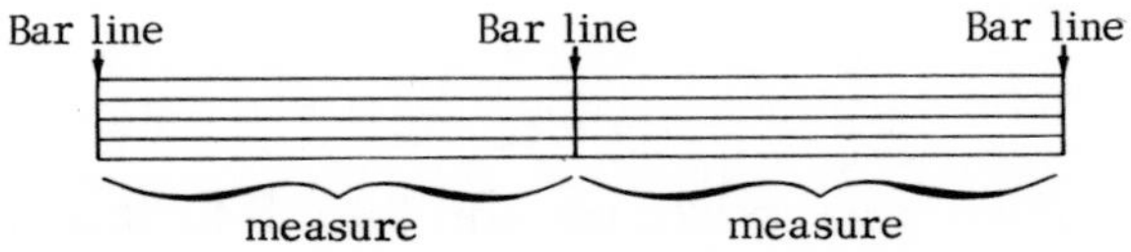

When there are two quarter notes in a measure the *time signature* will be $\frac{2}{4}$ ("two-four"). This time signature is written at the beginning of the piece and, unless specifically indicated elsewhere, applies to every measure in the piece.

Two-four time $\frac{2}{4}$ is the most basic metrical arrangement of beats within a musical measure. We walk, run and breathe in $\frac{2}{4}$.

When playing a piece in $\frac{2}{4}$, start by counting slowly and evenly "one-two one-two one-two . . ." before beginning. Give each "one" a slightly stronger emphasis than "two." Maintain the beat and make sure that the notes you are playing fall on their proper beats.

The following exercises are made up of notes on all the six strings and are written in $\frac{2}{4}$.

Notes on the E (First) String

Important: In the following exercises when reaching from a note on one fret to a note on a higher fret do not release the original finger from the lower fret.

This exercise is made up of notes on the first string. Play the notes with the first and second fingers of the right hand alternating.

Notes on the B (Second) String

This exercise is made up of notes on the first and second strings. Continue the alternation of the first and second fingers of the right hand.

Notes on the G (Third) String

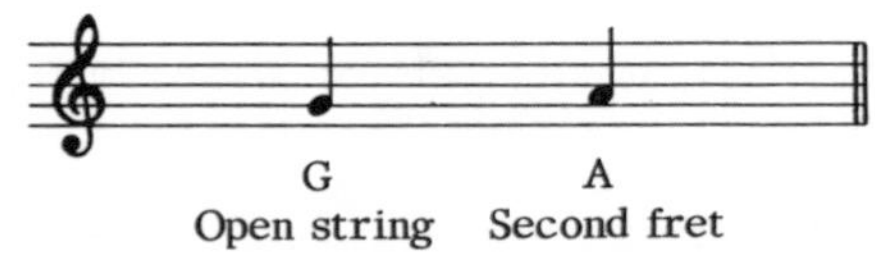

This exercise is made up of notes on the first three strings. Continue the alternation of the first and second fingers of the right hand.

Notes on the D (Fourth) String

This exercise is made up of notes on the first four strings. Use the right thumb to play the notes on the D string and continue the alternation of the first and second fingers on the first three strings as before.

Notes on the A (Fifth) String

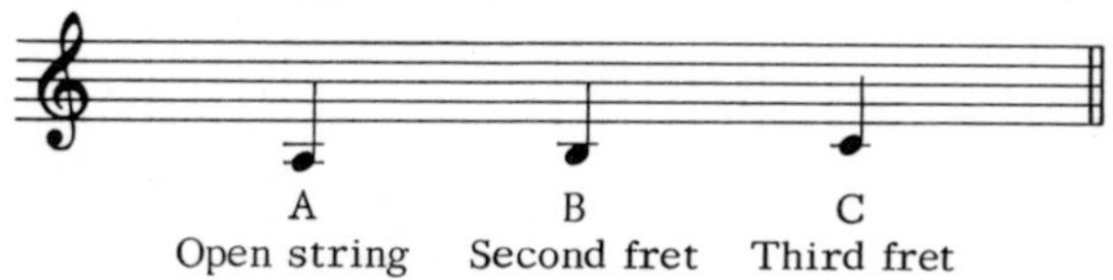

This exercise is made up of notes on the first five strings. Use the right thumb to play the notes on the A and D strings and continue the alternation of the first and second fingers on the first three strings as before.

Notes on the E (Sixth) String

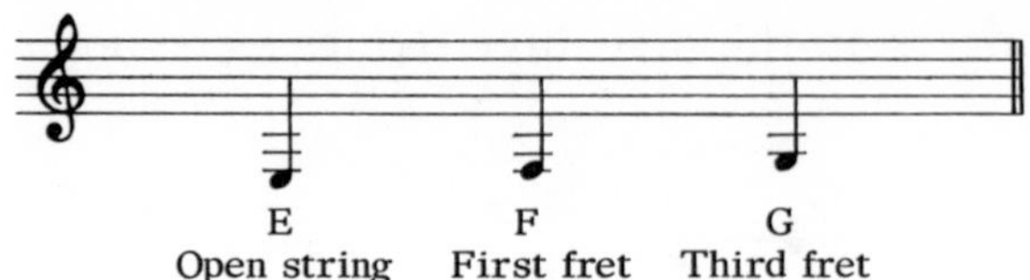

This exercise is made up of notes on all six strings. Use the right thumb to play the notes on the E, A, and D strings and continue the alternation of the first and second fingers on the first three strings as before.

Rhythm – Half and Whole Notes

Four-Quarter $\left(\frac{4}{4}\right)$ *Time*

A note whose total time duration is equal to two quarter notes is called a *half note.*

Half note = Quarter + Quarter

A note whose total time duration is equal to four quarter notes is called a *whole note.*

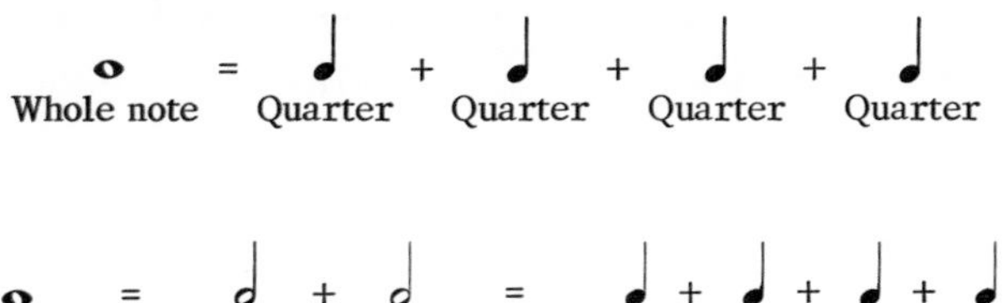

A period of silence is called a *rest.* There are corresponding rests for every note value.

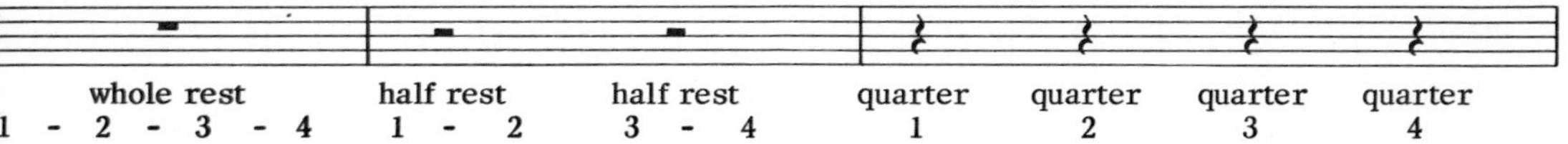

When the measures of a piece of music have four beats the piece is in four-quarter time $\frac{4}{4}$. In four-quarter (also called "four-four") time the first and the third beats usually get somewhat heavier accents than the second and fourth.

We Shall Overcome

Three-Quarter $\left(\frac{3}{4}\right)$ *Time*

We have had songs already where there were three beats per measure (*My Bonny Lies Over the Ocean, Home on the Range,* etc.). To write a note whose total time duration is equal to three quarter notes we must introduce a new musical symbol: the *dot.* A dot coming after a note increases that note's value by one half its original value. Thus, a dotted half note would be equal to a half plus half of a half—that is, a quarter—or, a total time value of three quarters.

1 - 2 - 3 = 1 - 2 + 3 = 1 + 2 + 3

If the time duration of a note extends beyond the confines of one measure we write that note again in the next measure and join the two notes (of the same pitch) with a curved line known as a *tie.* Only the first note of the tied pair is played. The counting is then continued for the total time of the tied notes.

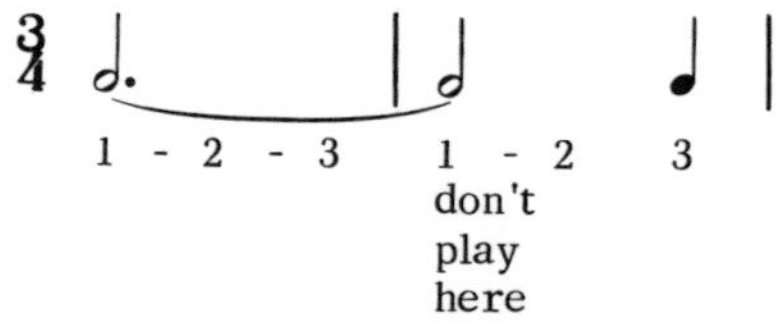

On Top of Old Smoky

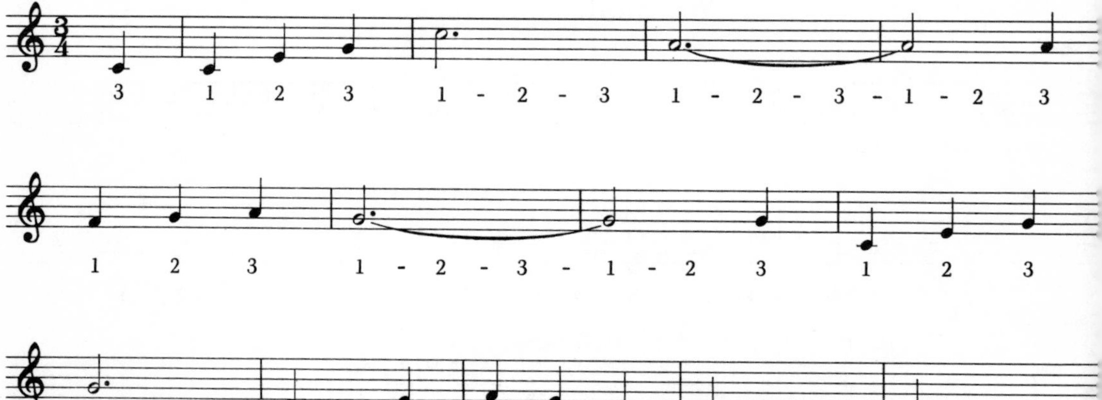

The Eighth Note

A note whose time duration is equal to half a quarter note is called an *eighth note.* Eighth notes may be written singly or in groups.

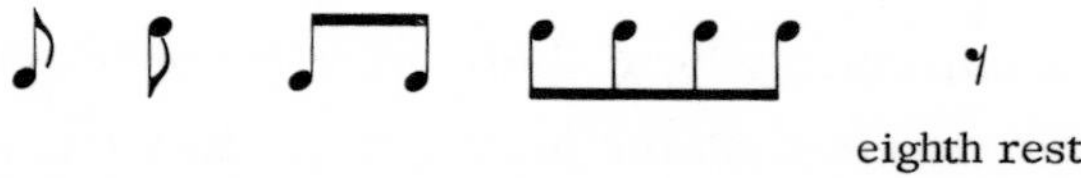

eighth rest

To time the playing of eighth notes properly we must subdivide the basic "one-two one-two . . ." of the quarter notes into the exactly twice as fast "one-and-two-and one-and-two-and . . ." of the eighth notes.

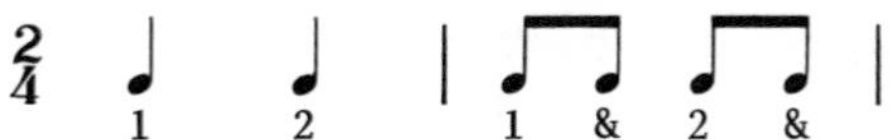

Black-Eyed Susie

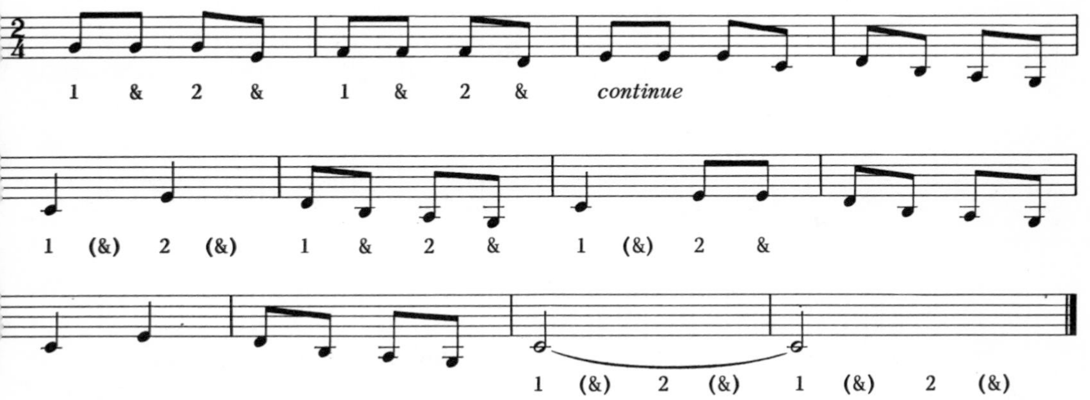

The Dotted Quarter Note

A dotted quarter note is equal in time to three eighth notes.

♩. = ♩ + ♪ = ♪ + ♪ + ♪

1 & 2

It may be found in music in $\frac{2}{4}$, $\frac{4}{4}$, and $\frac{3}{4}$.

Hold the Fort

The Streets of Laredo

Six-Eight $\left(\frac{6}{8}\right)$ *Time*

When the unit of beat is the eighth note and there are six eighth notes per measure the piece is in $\frac{6}{8}$. In $\frac{6}{8}$ the eighth note gets one count and the quarter note gets two. Usually the accent falls on the first and fourth eighth notes.

Irish Washerwoman

The Sixteenth Note

Four sixteenth notes equal one quarter note (or two eighth notes). Sixteenth notes may appear singly but more often they come in pairs or sets of four.

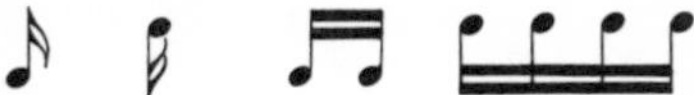

In order to time the playing of sixteenth notes properly we must subdivide the basic "one-two . . ." of the quarter notes or the twice as fast "one-and-two-and" of the eighth notes into the exactly four times as fast "one-uh-and-uh two-uh-and-uh" of the desired sixteenth notes.

1 2 3 4
1 & 2 & 3 & 4 &
1-uh-&-uh 2-uh-&-uh 3-uh-&-uh 4-uh-&-uh

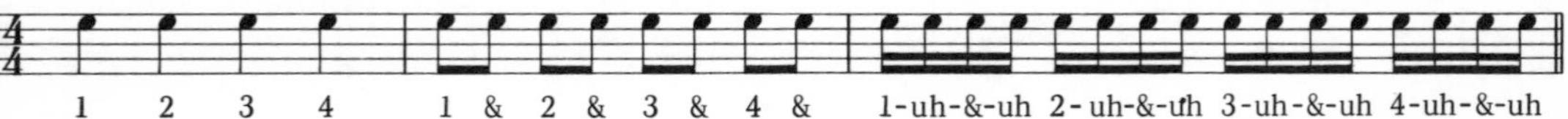

Soldier's Joy

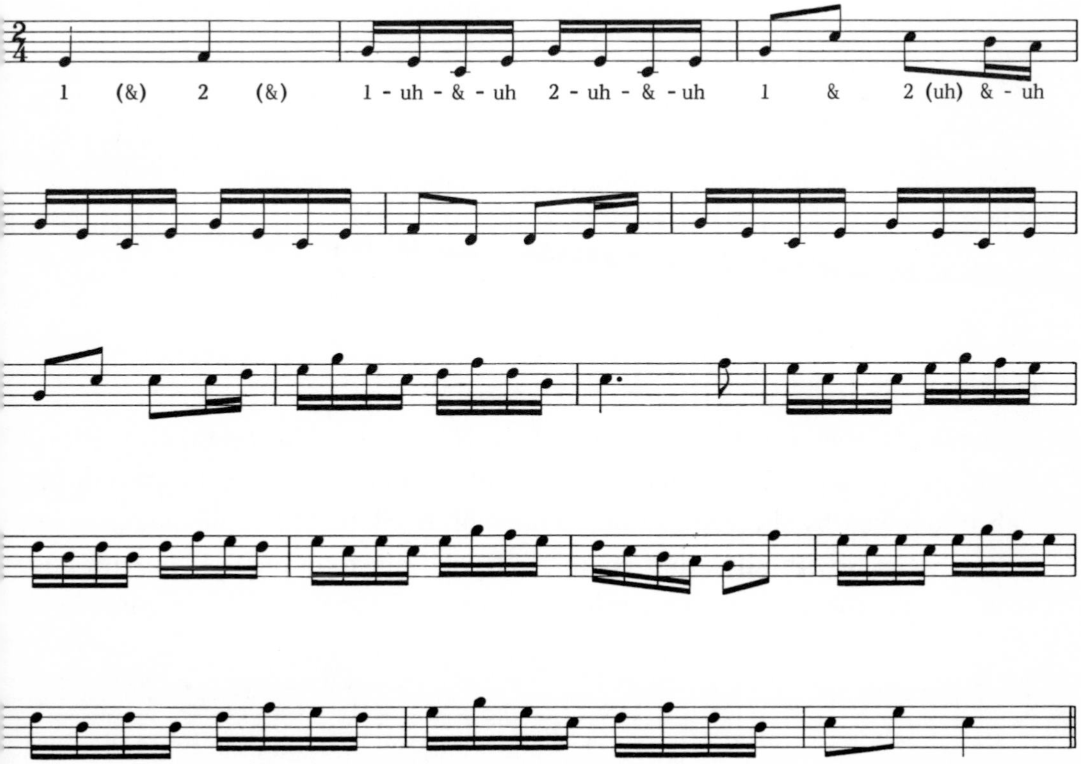

1 (&) 2 (&)
1 - uh - & - uh 2 - uh - & - uh
1 & 2 (uh) & - uh

Devil's Dream

The Dotted Eighth and Sixteenth

A dotted eighth is equal to three sixteenths. This note is usually followed by a sixteenth. The whole figure, then, equals one quarter.

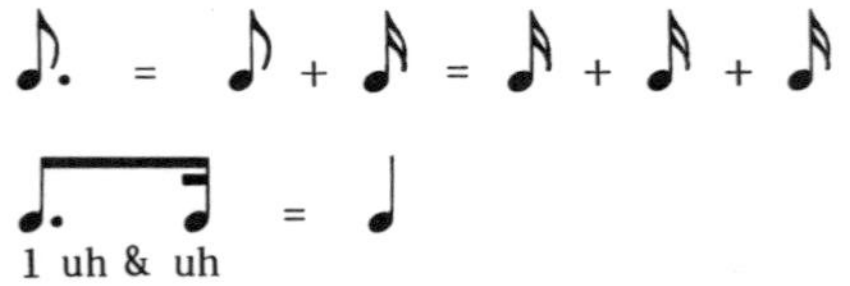

1 uh & uh

In the playing of music containing this figure care must be taken to give it the proper "snap." One must get the feel of the three-times-as-long dotted eighth followed by the very "short" sound of the sixteenth. Counting is as important here as with any other rhythmic figure, but too much of "one-uh-and-uh . . ." will tend to slow the music down beyond the point of recognition.

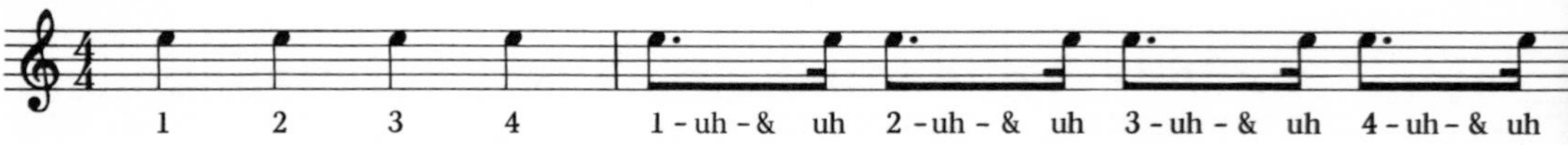

Tramp, Tramp, Tramp

The Triplet

If a quarter note is subdivided into three equal parts we have a *triplet.*

3
1 2 3 = 1-2-3

Tying together the first two eighth notes of the triplet we get the following figure.

3 3
1 2 3 = 1 - 2 3 =

Remember that because of the triplet sign this "quarter" and "eighth" combination adds up to one quarter note. We started by subdividing a quarter note—so we still have the original quarter note value under the triplet bracket. This rhythmic figure sounds something like the dotted eighth sixteenth combination but there is a difference. Here the first note gets two counts to the second note's one. With the dotted eighth and sixteenth the ratio of first to second note is three to one.

These triplet figures occur very often in blues.

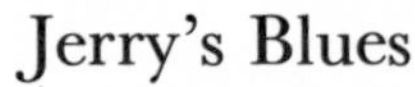

Accidentals: Sharps and Flats

The notes comprising the exercises and songs we have played up to now are what are called *natural notes.* They are by no means the only notes available to us. To play these other notes we need two additional symbols: the *sharp sign* and the *flat sign.*

♯	♭	♮
sharp	flat	natural cancels sharp or flat

A sharp sign appearing directly in front of a note raises that note by one fret.

A flat sign appearing directly in front of a note lowers that note by one fret.

Up to now we have played everything in a key with no sharps or flats—the key of C. Now we will take a look at some of the keys that folk guitarists play in, other than C.

The Key of G Major

The key of G major has a *key signature* of one sharp—F sharp.

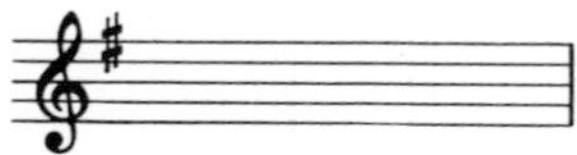

This key signature of F sharp applies to each and every note F that may appear in the piece subsequently—high or low. F sharp is played at the following frets.

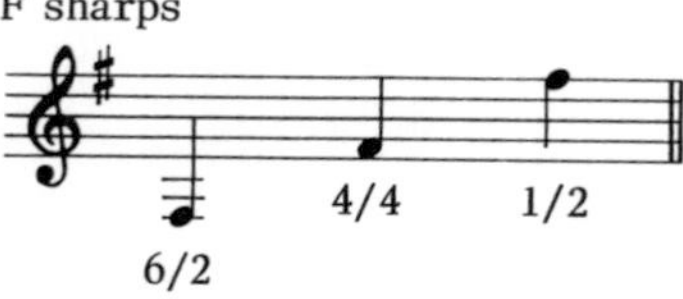

Here is the G-major scale.

Gee, But I Want to Go Home

Paper of Pins

Play the songs in the previous sections of the book which are in the key of G.

The Key of D Major

The key of D major has a key signature of two sharps—F sharp and C sharp. C sharp is played at the following frets.

C sharps

Here is the D-major scale.

Blue-tail Fly

On Springfield Mountain

Play the songs in the previous sections of the book which are in the key of D.

The Key of A Major

The key of A major has a key signature of three sharps—F sharp, C sharp, and G sharp. G sharp is played at the following frets.

Here is the A-major scale.

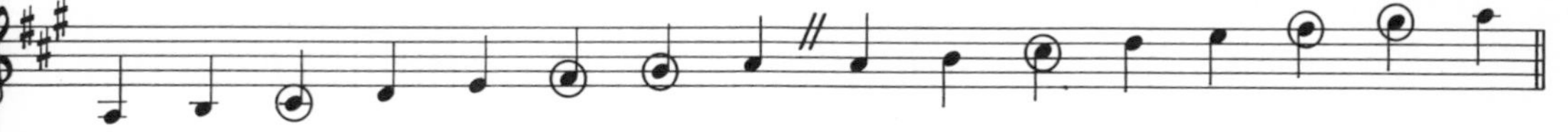

The Sow Took the Measles

Villikins and His Dinah

Play the songs in the previous sections of the book which are in the key of A.

The Key of E Major

The key of E major has a key signature of four sharps—F sharp, C sharp, G sharp, and D sharp. D sharp is played at the following frets.

Here is the E-major scale.

A-Roving

Barbara Allen

Play the songs in the previous sections of the book which are in the key of E.

This completes the basic five keys (C,G,D,A,E) generally encountered in folk guitar arrangements. In addition there is one other major key which is occasionally used.

The Key of F Major

The key of F major has a key signature of one flat—B flat. B flat is played at the following frets.

Here is the F-major scale.

The Grey Goose

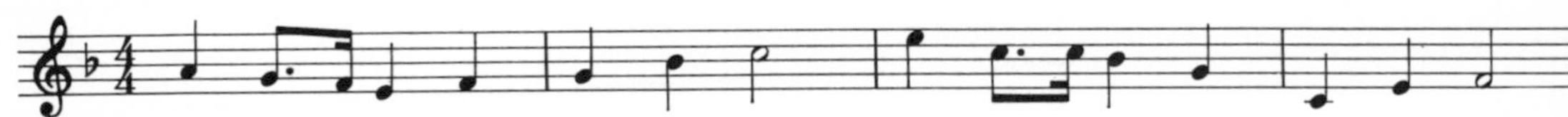

The Foggy, Foggy Dew

Before considering the remaining keys it will be useful to study the following *chromatic scales* containing all the sharps and all the flats fret by fret.

The Chromatic Scale with Sharps

The Chromatic Scale with Flats

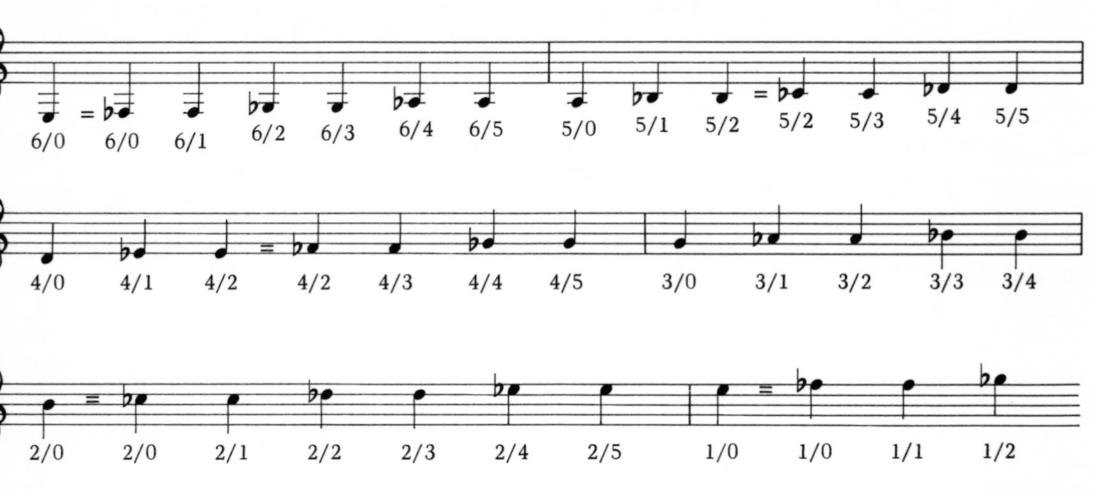

The Remaining Sharp Keys

The Remaining Flat Keys

E♭ major
A♭ major
D♭ major
G♭ major
C♭ major

TUNING THE GUITAR

Tuning any instrument is a process of trial and error. It involves comparing a standard pitch with the note you are trying to tune and making the necessary adjustments in that note. The degree of accuracy in tuning depends upon your ability to hear small differences in pitch. This ability is present in varying degrees of refinement in different people. It can be sharpened, to some extent, by exposure to the tuning process itself and by "knowing what to listen for."

The pitch of a string—on a guitar, for example—is dependent upon three factors, two of which are variable and one which is relatively fixed. The variables are the length and the tension of the string, the fixed factor is the string's diameter.

If you shorten the vibrating length of a string by pressing down at some fret, the pitch will rise proportionately. If you lengthen the same string by pressing down at a lower fret or playing the string open again, the pitch will fall.

If you tighten a string by turning the tuning peg, the pitch will rise. Loosening the string, by turning the peg in the opposite direction, lowers the pitch.

As far as changing the diameter is concerned, this can be done, obviously, only by playing another string. The smaller the diameter the higher the pitch—the greater the diameter the lower the pitch.

There are a number of practical ways to tune the guitar.

The guitar may be tuned to a piano. If this is done you must be aware of the fact that the strings of the guitar sound an octave lower than they are usually written. The relationship between guitar strings and piano keys is the following:

Remember, though, that even if you play the same notes on the piano as on the guitar *a piano will not sound like a guitar.* This difference in tonal quality (*timbre*) may be confusing at first but it can be overcome. A good way to bridge the gap between the two instruments is to sing or hum the desired note and tune the guitar to your voice. While there is a difference between the timbres of piano, voice, and guitar, once we really hear the pitch "inside" ourselves we have taken a great step forward in the tuning process.

A *guitar pitchpipe* will give the actual pitch of the six strings.

If no standard pitch is available the guitar may be tuned *relative to itself.* This is the most basic way of tuning the instrument and it requires the most careful listening. It can only be attempted after you have had some experience playing and have some idea of what an "in tune" instrument sounds like.

The best way to begin tuning using this process (or indeed any other method) is first to determine if your instrument is out of tune. If you cannot tell by playing the open strings then play an E minor chord slowly—string by string. Listen closely for any note that may seem out of order. If a string seems off you must decide whether it is too high or too low and then tighten or loosen it according to your determination.

If the sixth (E) string seems to be all right you can make the following check on the others:

The *fifth fret* of the sixth string is A. This should sound the same as the fifth string.

The *fifth fret* of the fifth string is D. This should sound the same as the fourth string.

The *fifth fret* of the fourth string is G. This should sound the same as the third string.

The *fourth fret* of the third string is B. This should sound the same as the second string.

The *fifth fret* of the second string is E. This should sound the same as the first string.

The first string (E) should then be compared with the sixth string (E—two octaves lower).

Play a few chords string by string and listen closely—you may have to repeat this tuning process a number of times before you are completely satisfied.

Another relative pitch method involves tuning the open strings to each other. This is done by "hearing" the musical interval between adjacent strings. E–A, A–D, D–G, B–E are *perfect fourths.* G–B is a *major third.*

A perfect fourth may be sung easily if you think of the first two notes of *When Johnny Comes Marching Home, Home on the Range, Aura Lee, Funiculi, Funicula, Froggie Went A-Courting*, *Taps,* and many other songs.

A major third may be sung easily if you think of the first two notes of *Michael, Row the Boat Ashore, Kum Ba Ya, When I First Came to This Land,* and many others. You can even play part of *Taps* on the D, G, and B strings to check on their tuning.

Transposing

A piece of music or a song may be played and sung in any key. In the learning of chords and instrumental technique you may have found that some of the songs which illustrated the material were either too high or too low for you. The keys of these songs may be changed (*transposed*) to more comfortable ones depending upon your voice.

Most simple folk songs can be harmonized by using three chords. For example: C, F, G7 or D, G, A7. If you check back at the scales you will see that these chords are based on the first, fourth, and fifth notes of their respective keys. These I, IV, and V chords are the backbone of our musical system. Any song starting with C could just as well start with D, G, or any other note providing the relationship among the following chords is maintained.

Table of I, IV, and $V_{(7)}$ Chords

KEY	I	IV	V(7)
C	C	F	G
G	G	C	D
D	D	G	A
A	A	D	E
E	E	A	B
B	B	E	F♯
F♯ (G♭)	F♯ (G♭)	B (C♭)	C♯ (D♭)
C♯ (D♭)	C♯ (D♭)	F♯ (G♭)	G♯ (A♭)
A♭	A♭	D♭	E♭
E♭	E♭	A♭	B♭
B♭	B♭	E♭	F
F	F	B♭	C

The I chord is called the *tonic,* the IV, the *subdominant,* the V, the *dominant.*

As you know, these three chords are not the only chords found in many songs. The number of possibilities is virtually unlimited—depending upon the style and period of the music. The process of transposition, however, remains the same: Determine the relationship between the chords in the original key and then substitute chords with the same relationship in the new key.

Remember the key signatures when transposing. C major is the only key without sharps or flats—and the chords in C reflect this.

All other keys will have at least one chord with a sharp or flat in its spelling. The following table will illustrate chords for the six common folk guitar keys.

Key				*Chords*			
	I	II	III	IV	V	VI	VIII
C	C	Dm	Em	F	G	Am	B dim
G	G	Am	Bm	C	D	Em	F♯dim
D	D	Em	F♯m	G	A	Bm	C♯dim
A	A	Bm	C♯m	D	E	F♯m	G♯dim
E	E	F♯m	G♯m	A	B	C♯m	D♯dim
F	F	Gm	Am	B♭	C	Dm	E dim

The Capo

For playing characteristic, graceful folk style accompaniments in all keys a *capo* is highly recommended. The capo is an elastic or metal clamp that fits over all the strings at a particular fret and raises the pitch of the guitar by that many frets (half steps). In effect, it transposes the guitar.

If a song in the key of G, say, is too low for you—try putting the capo on the third fret. This will give you the key of B flat. You should refer to the chromatic scales on page 199 to see what new chords are arrived at by moving familiar chords up by means of a capo. (C up one fret is C sharp, up three frets is E flat—and so on.)

BASIC GUITAR CHORDS

Key to symbols employed in this chart:

P = Primary Bass String
A = Alternate Bass String
x = String Not To Be Played
o = Open String To Be Played
③ = Finger May Be Moved For Alternate Bass
⌒ = Barre

Note: The numbers immediately to the right of some of the diagrams indicate the fret at which the chord is to begin.

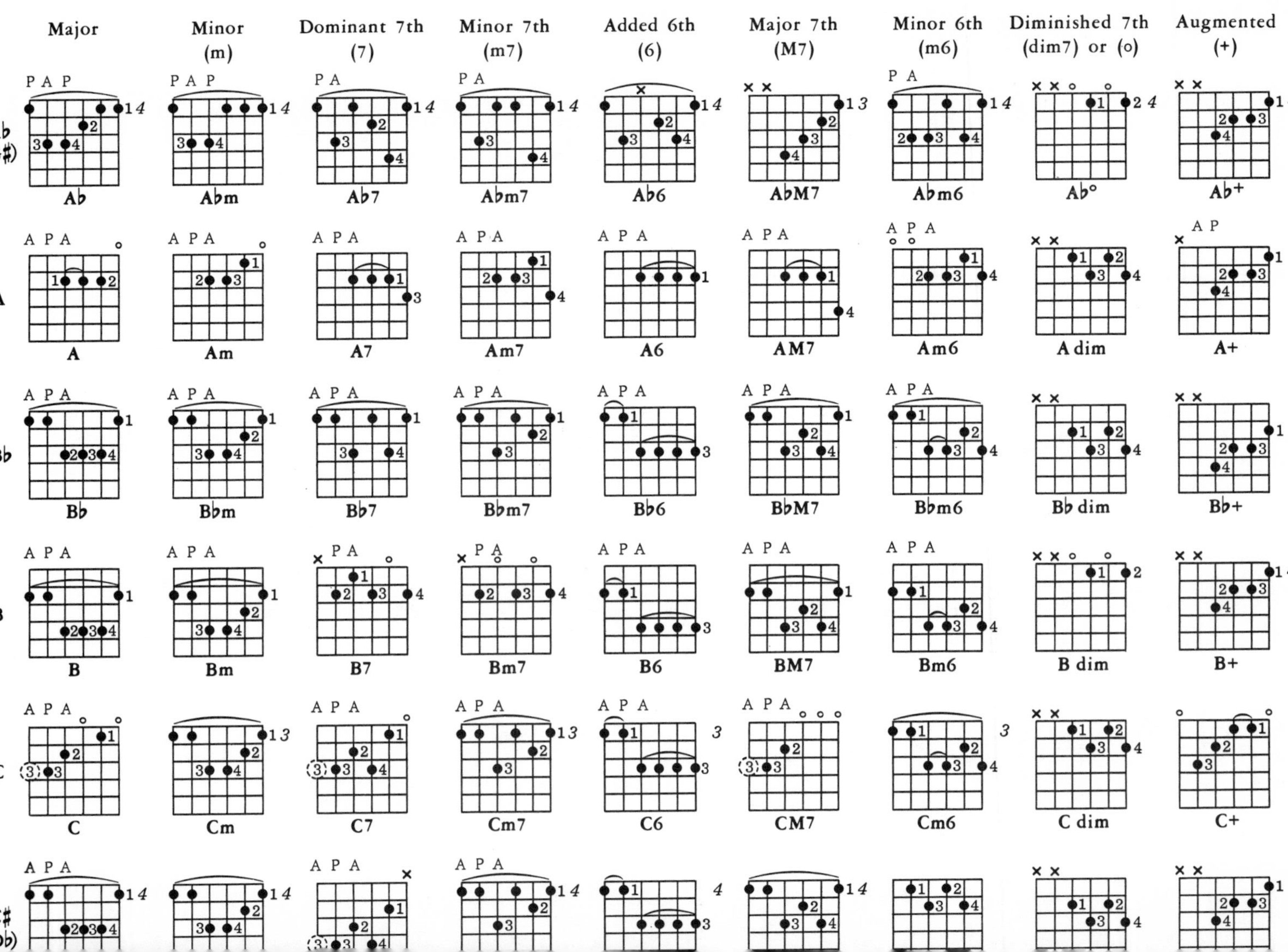

Major
Minor (m)
Dominant 7th (7)
Minor 7th (m7)
Added 6th (6)
Major 7th (M7)
Minor 6th (m6)
Diminished 7th (dim7) or (o)
Augmented (+)
A♭ (G♯)
A♭ A♭m A♭7 A♭m7 A♭6 A♭M7 A♭m6 A♭° A♭+
A
A Am A7 Am7 A6 AM7 Am6 A dim A+
B♭
B♭ B♭m B♭7 B♭m7 B♭6 B♭M7 B♭m6 B♭ dim B♭+
B
B Bm B7 Bm7 B6 BM7 Bm6 B dim B+
C
C Cm C7 Cm7 C6 CM7 Cm6 C dim C+
C♯ (D♭)

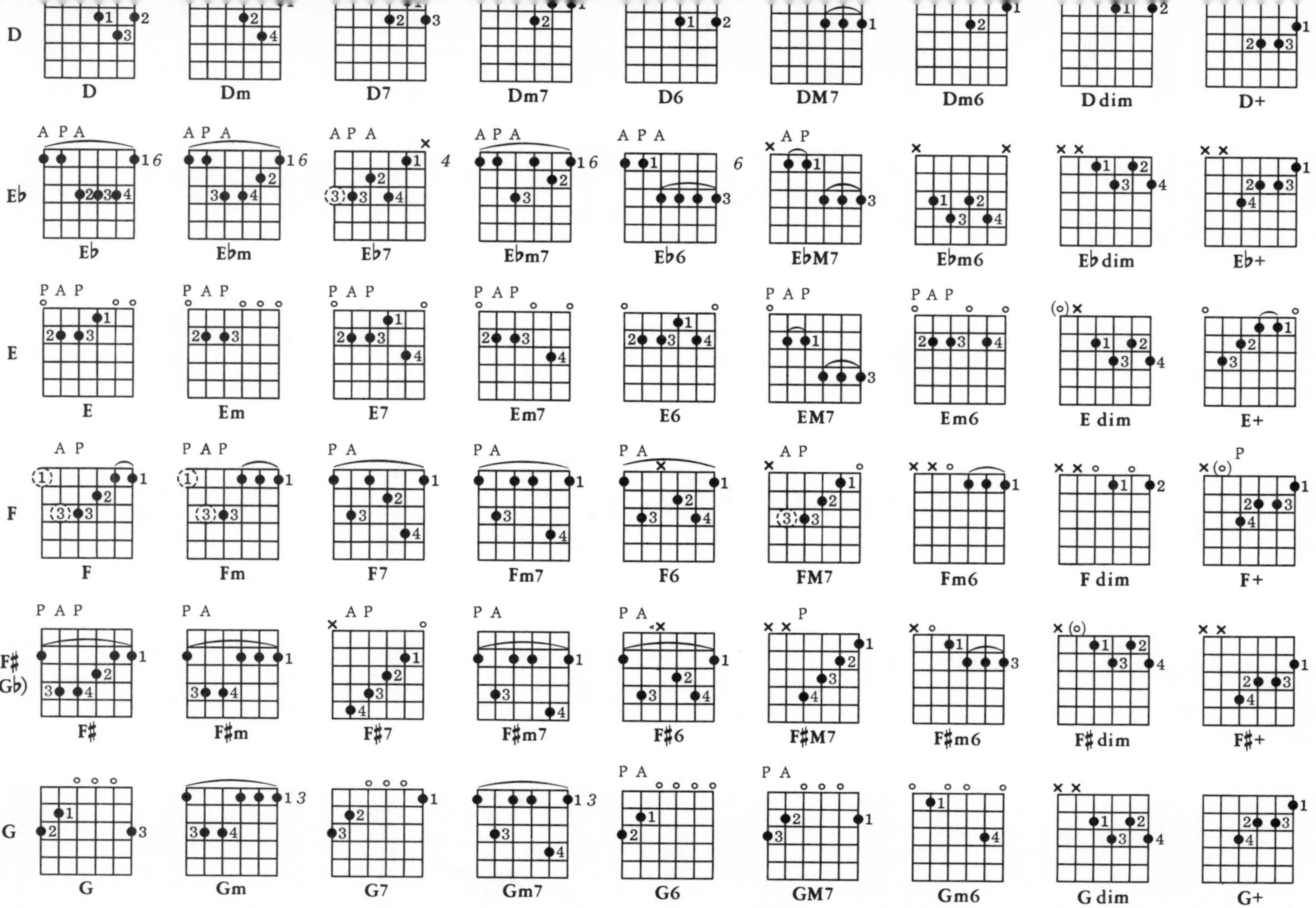
D
D Dm D7 Dm7 D6 DM7 Dm6 D dim D+
E♭
E♭ E♭m E♭7 E♭m7 E♭6 E♭M7 E♭m6 E♭ dim E♭+
E
E Em E7 Em7 E6 EM7 Em6 E dim E+
F
F Fm F7 Fm7 F6 FM7 Fm6 F dim F+
F♯ (G♭)
F♯ F♯m F♯7 F♯m7 F♯6 F♯M7 F♯m6 F♯ dim F♯+
G
G Gm G7 Gm7 G6 GM7 Gm6 G dim G+